W9-CIM-106

SENIOR HIGH VOL. 10
Pacesetter

COMPLETE YOUTH MINISTRY RESOURCE

Identity Search

FINDING WHO I AM AS GOD'S SPECIAL CHILD

■

David C. Cook Publishing Co.

Elgin, Illinois/Weston, Ontario

Senior High PACESETTER

■

IDENTITY SEARCH
Finding Who I Am As God's Special Child

DAVID C. COOK PUBLISHING CO.
Elgin, Illinois/Weston, Ontario
IDENTITY SEARCH
Finding Who I Am As God's Special Child

■

Creative Team

Project Editor: John Duckworth
Editors: Anne E. Dinnan; Paul N. Woods
Associate Editor: Eric Potter
Designer: Jill E. Novak, Russ Peterson

■

Management Team

David C. Cook III, Editor in Chief
Ralph Gates, Director of Church Resources
Marlene D. LeFever, Executive Editor of Church Resources
Jim Townsend, Bible Editor
Randy Maid, Director of Design Services

■

We'd like to thank the many encouragers who helped PACESETTER become reality.—The Editors
Published by David C. Cook Publishing. Co.
850 North Grove Avenue
Elgin, Illinois 60120
Cable address: DCCOOK
First printing, 1987
Printed in the United States of America
Library of Congress Catalog.Number: 86-72969
ISBN: 1-5551-794-6

Identity Search

FINDING WHO I AM AS GOD'S SPECIAL CHILD

See, it's very hard for me to share my feelings," a teenager said. "I'm afraid that if people really know me they won't like me."

The youth worker who heard that statement nodded—and winced. She knew how that teen felt because she'd been there, too. Most of us have.

Adolescence is a time of trying on different identities, of trying to put the pieces together. And kids are not entirely sure they'll like what they find. How can they expect anybody *else* to like them? Our acceptance of them, through all their craziness, can give them confidence that perhaps there is someone worthwhile inside waiting to be discovered.

That requires being open about who *we* are—saying, "I don't like everything about myself, but I'm not afraid to let you know who I am. That's because I think I'm okay. I like myself." This is hard-won maturity that comes from feeling God's (and other people's) love.

The fact that God knows us—our strange feelings, our weaknesses, the impulses that so often frighten us—and loves us anyway, is very good news indeed. The Scriptures promise that we shall know, even as we are known (I Corinthians 13:12).

No wonder people, whatever their ages, never get tired of singing,

Yes, Jesus loves me. Yes, Jesus loves me.
Yes, Jesus loves me. The Bible tells me so.

INSIDE · THIS · VOLUME

Identity Search (Volume 10 in the PACESETTER series) can help you guide your kids to self-understanding and acceptance as unique and valued children of God.

For your own background and enrichment, we offer you "Expert Insights," articles by leaders in youth ministry and counseling. For example, Keith Olson, author of *Counseling Teenagers,* explains how forming an identity is the chief task of adolescence. Then Barbara Varenhorst, founder and director of the Palo Alto Peer Counseling Center, writes warmly about how to help kids accept themselves and others. Finally, Donald Joy, professor of human de-

velopment and author of *Bonding: Relationships in the Image of God,* explains how an adolescent's sexual development fuels growth to emotional and spiritual maturity.

Then, use PACESETTER's practical programming tools:

■ The "Meetings" section gives you five complete meeting plans for helping kids develop healthy self-concepts. Reproduce the activity pieces at the back of this book for use with these meetings.

■ In the "More Bright Ideas" section, you'll find about 20 activity ideas, many suitable as meetings in themselves. Use these ideas whenever you need them.

■ Need material for an upcoming retreat? You'll find it in "Breakaway." The theme is affirming what's special about your young people.

■ "Kids in the Spotlight" offers drama with a light touch—a humorous skit on identity by Steve and Annie Wamberg.

■ Finally, to help you build a solid and caring youth group, we've included a section called, "Nurturing Your Group."

So if you're looking at a blank calendar and wondering what you're going to do, you've come to the right place. Whether you need one activity or months of programming, PACESETTER is at your service. □

Contents

Contents

Identity Search:

A the task of dolescence

Virtually everything an adolescent does is related to the forming of identity.

"Then God said, 'Let us make man in our image, in our likeness, and let them rule over the fish of the sea and the birds of the air, over the livestock, over all the earth, and over all the creatures that move along the ground.' So God created man in his own image, in the image of God he created him; male and female he created them" (Genesis 1:26, 27). As God formed Adam from the dust and breathed the breath of life into his nostrils, the parameters of man's identity were established. Man was created to reflect the identity of God. It might be more accurately stated that instead of *forming* our identity, we *find* our identity in an expression of God's nature. Since we are finite and God is infinite, each of us can only partially reflect His image.

It is during the adolescent stage of life (approximately between 12 and 21 years) that a person's primary psychological task is to form (or find) his or her identity. Virtually everything teenagers do relates directly to their identity development. Their rebellion against parents and other authority figures plays a major role in identity formation. So does the emphasis on belonging to peer groups and developing more intimate relationships with special friends of the opposite sex. The vast differences between squirmy junior highs and thoughtful college seniors is understood partially through the concept of identity formation. Youth ministers, Sunday school teachers, and parents will know much more about why their adolescents act as they do when they realize that their behavior is all part of developing identity.

BY G. KEITH OLSON

Components of Identity

What is identity? When psychologists say that the primary psychological task of adolescence is identity development, what are they talking about? Breaking down the concept of identity into four of its components will help us to better understand.

The first of these components is *self-concept*. Who am I? What am I really like? What makes me different from everyone else? Is there anything about me that makes being me special? These are some of the important questions a young person needs to answer to develop a self-concept. During these teenage years more than at any other time, individuals are overwhelmingly concerned about who they really are. There is an all-encompassing need to discover a common thread that links together all of the roles they play with people.

In a conversation with his youth pastor, 14-year-old George told him, "Look, I'm a student, a son, a brother, a baseball player on my

> ## "Am I just a collection of all those roles?"

team, a friend with my neighbors, a member of our youth group at church, and a boyfriend to Susan. But who am I? Am I just a collec-

tion of all those roles? I don't know if there is anything about me that puts all of that together. You know what I mean? Who's George?" This freshman boy is struggling to develop a self-concept.

Self-ideal is a second component of identity. It is formed in order to answer a different set of questions. Who do I most want to be like? What personal characteristics do I most want to possess? How do I want people to remember me? These and similar questions are answered by the person's self-ideal.

Barbara's parents took her to a counselor when she was a junior in high school. She was depressed, and her mind was filled with self-rejecting, demeaning thoughts: "If only I could be like my older sister. She's so pretty and popular. Everybody loves her. All the kids know her. And she gets along so well with Mom and Dad, too." Further probing revealed more of the characteristics that Barbara thought made her sister so wonderful. These traits, then, had become central to her self-ideal.

For some teenagers, the self-ideal is a person. It may be a movie star, an outstanding athlete, parent, rock star, or minister. For other young people, the self-ideal is a list of personal traits, talents, and characteristics they would ideally like to possess. Many young people have quite lofty self-ideals. Adolescence is a time of strong idealism, and many teens set personal goals so high that they are quite difficult and sometimes impossible to reach.

Self-evaluation is a third component of identity and emerges from the combination of self-concept and self-ideal. The teenager's self-evaluation answers still another set of questions. How do I feel about myself? How well do I like being me? Do my good qualities outweigh my weaker characteristics? Psychologists and counselors find that when

people's self-concepts are not too far from their self-ideals, their self-evaluations are likely to be quite positive. When there is a great gap between self-concept and self-ideal, however, people usually feel more negative about themselves.

> # Help kids narrow the gap between their real and ideal self-concepts.

We met George during our discussion of self-concept. As a freshman in high school he was struggling with developing his concept of who he really was. During the discussion with his youth pastor he was asked to think about the kind of person he really wanted to be. He made two columns on a piece of paper, labeling one, "Who I am," and the other, "How I wish to be." After completing his list, George could see that the way he saw himself that day was not too different from his ideal self. George had the reputation of being a generally happy and contented young person.

Barbara, whom we also met earlier, presented a very different picture. She was depressed and discouraged. Her grades at school were deteriorating and she was becoming more socially isolated from her friends. She was also extremely rebellious and uncooperative at home. Barbara's counselor helped her to recognize that her self-concept was very limited and quite negative. She was also able to see that there was a great gulf between the way she saw herself and her self-ideal. Counseling helped Barbara to gain a more positive and realistic concept of who she really was. She was able to see and admit that she possessed more positive traits. She was also helped to reevaluate her self-ideal. She had seen her sister as if the latter wore a halo, and that was far from the truth. Bringing more realism to her perception of herself and her self-ideal raised her self-evaluation.

We can learn from Barbara's counselor. As you work with teenagers who exhibit negative self-evaluations, ask yourself two questions: (1) How do they describe themselves? (2) How do they wish they could ideally be? Then evaluate the degree of reality in both their self-concepts and self-ideals. Finally, help them narrow the gap between their real and ideal self-concepts. In some cases the majority of the work should be directed toward helping the adolescent elevate his or her self-concept. Others require more effort to enable them to lower their self-ideals to more attainable levels.

A fourth component of identity is the *self as locus of power.* This concept refers to the degree of power or control the teenager has over his or her life. Remember the image in which people were created. God's image is one of vast power and authority, and He created us to reflect that power. "Then God said, 'Let us make man in our image . . . and let them rule over the fish of the sea and the birds of the air, over the livestock, over all the earth, and over all the creatures

that move along the ground' " (Genesis 1:26). God wants us to develop power and control over ourselves so we can then "rule" with wisdom and integrity in the world.

A vital part of identity formation, then, is becoming people who possess personal power, and who recognize that power. Teenagers need to learn how to wisely use the power they are developing. Youth ministers and sponsors work with adolescents who vary widely in their ability to control and constructively use their power. One local youth worker, for example, recently spent many hours counseling with the parents of a 16-year-old boy who ran away from home. By running away, this boy vividly demonstrated to his parents just how much power he possessed. But he did it in a very hurtful and destructive way.

> # Teenagers need to learn how to wisely use the power they are developing.

Other teenagers are slow to develop power in themselves. Their lives are still controlled by external forces. Some of these young peo-

ple actively fight against becoming more powerful; it is just too frightening for them to think of having more control and responsibility for their lives. They are more comfortable in childhood dependency on parents, teachers, and other authority figures.

Valerie, for instance, was afraid to grow into more maturity and responsibility when she was first seen in counseling. Though quite bright, she purposely worked only for average and below-average grades. She was well liked in her youth group, but shrank from any leadership roles. Instead of initiating activities with friends, she typically waited to be invited. Young people like Valerie need help and encouragement so they can gradually become more self-reliant. From a spiritual perspective, these teenagers need to grow in their trust in the Spirit of Christ who indwells them.

How Identity Develops

Psychologist Erik H. Erikson has offered valuable insight into understanding how people grow. His concept of developmental psychology suggests that people are continually growing or developing throughout their lives. There are several stages of development, and each stage has a primary psychological developmental task. Adolescence is understood to be one phase or segment in this ongoing growth process. Identity formation is the developmental task which is so vital to healthy adolescent growth.

Here are six tenets of developmental psychology which will help you to understand more clearly how your young people are progressing in their identity formation:

1. Their earlier life experiences are having an impact on their present lives. Their current work at forming an identity is affected by

what has occurred before.

2. Their current life experience will have an impact on their future lives. Their future work at forming an identity will be affected by what is occurring now.

3. Experiences which occur earlier in life have a more profound effect on future development than experiences which occur later. Expect your young people to be more affected by experiences which occurred during their early childhoods than they are by later childhood experiences.

4. The path of psychological development goes from general to specific. As teenagers grow through the adolescent years their sense of identity becomes more clearly defined.

5. Developmental changes build on each other to form a specific direction of growth. Adolescent identity traits become stronger or more pronounced as young people grow through their teenage years.

6. Since growth and development are never completed, changes in the direction of growth are always possible. Teenagers' negative identities can be altered to become more positive through your help. Unfortunately, their positive identities can also be altered to become more negative through a series of destructive influences.

Those of you who work with junior high, high schoolers, and college-age young people know that there are vast differences among these groups. They are all adolescents, but they are at different stages in their adolescent development. A brief look at these three stages helps to reveal how young people are working to develop their identities as they pass through adolescence.

Early adolescence begins just before puberty and lasts approximately one and a half to two years, generally from about ages 12 to 14.

These young people are pushing away from parental influence and are aligning themselves with their peer group. Friends become the primary source of influence. They develop "buddy" relationships, especially with same-sex friends. Secondary sexual characteristics caused by puberty bring dramatic changes in their bodies, which in turn change the way others respond to them. Changes occur in their own self-perceptions as well.

Mid-adolescence usually lasts from about 14 to 16 years of age. These teenagers continue to push away from parents, often joining groups that are different and sometimes contradictory to their parents' wishes. This pushing away from

> # Changes in the direction of growth are always possible.

parents helps adolescents to see themselves as individuals, separate and different from their parents. Their peer relationships are changing from the earlier group emphasis toward a focus on selecting special individual friends. Close bonds are formed with same-sex friends and romantic ties are usually formed with members of the opposite sex.

Late adolescence usually begins at about age 17 and lasts until approximately 19 to 21. Relationships with parents and other authority figures begin to normalize. Selected friendships with age peers continue, and more intimate relationships with the opposite sex develop. During this transition stage into young adulthood, young people become more focused on future issues. Greater responsibility for their lives is accepted and career orientations are developed.

All of these changes and developments that occur during the three stages of adolescence are central to the formation of healthy identity. Parenting, teaching, youth programming, and counseling should each be designed and carried out to support all of these activities. As we work together we can help our young people to develop (or find) their identities as individuals created to reflect the image of God. □

Dr. Keith Olson *is a marriage, family, and child counselor. The founder and director of Family Consultation Service of San Diego, California, he leads workshops in counseling skills for students, pastors, and lay workers, and is the author of* Counseling Teenagers *(Group Books).*

Advertising Man Tells How Ads Affect Teen Identity

Advertising's purpose is to sell products. Most of us realize that TV commercials and magazine ads, however clever and entertaining they may be, are simply sales presentations. That's not a problem in itself; at their best, ads show the variety of things we can choose to purchase.

But at its worst, advertising can leave us feeling as if we have no choice at all. Many teens feel the attitudes and lifestyles reflected in ads leave them little choice. Pressed by their friends, young people subconsciously adopt the norms of Madison Avenue—norms geared to sell products, not develop people. Because high schoolers have unstable self-images, advertising often becomes a strong reference point for them. Sales pitches can have the most effect in these areas in which youth are most vulnerable.

Here are three questions teens ask themselves—and which give advertisers a strong influence on teen development:

1. *"Who am I really?"* As teens struggle to balance their individuality with their need to fit in, ads tip the balance toward conformity. Commercial spokespersons, including popular stars, conveniently provide role models to follow. Ads for such products as fashions and music claim to sell individuality, but true individuality can't be mass-produced.

Why do advertisers foster this kind of dependence? Because mass marketing requires masses to buy the products. A tidal wave of support for "new" or "in" jeans, running shoes, or music groups translates into corporate profits. Advertisers know that word of mouth is the foremost reason people choose one product over another; that word can take the form of a simple personal recommendation or less subtle peer pressure. Setting a national standard of buying behavior sends approval-hungry teens to the cash registers.

2. *"How do others see me?"* The "peer" in peer pressure includes the imaginary crowd of classmates choreographed on TV commercial sound stages— as well as real-life friends. Thus products that appear on TV or in the press often seem like tickets to popularity. As one businessman said, "In our factory, we make lipstick. In our advertising, we sell hope."

Some kids even imitate the ads, hoping to transfer a commercial's popularity to themselves. They mimic an ad's humor or adopt "cool" or flirtatious attitudes they see on TV and in print.

3. *"What am I worth?"* High schoolers, wondering about love, friendship, and physical attractiveness, often get the wrong impression from ads. Advertising focuses on external qualities, creating a superficial way of evaluating people. Advertisers, thinking of products, talk about the best, the most, and the latest; teens can start to measure their bodies, relationships, and possessions against these superlatives and come up short.

U.S. teenagers spend about $30 billion a year on such "discretionary" items as clothes, makeup, records, and stereo equipment. That's no secret to advertisers. And that's why we need to educate kids about the assumptions behind many advertising campaigns. Exposure to various product choices may be beneficial, but trying to buy your way through fear and self-doubt is not.

—Chris Grant

Chris Grant *is advertising manager for* Christianity Today, *Inc.*

WHEN KIDS DON'T LIKE themselves

As the students shuffled and shoved

into the classroom, I groaned inside. Greg already was picking on the boy slumped in a chair next to him. Lori was laughing and giggling at every student who appeared. Steve had made a mocking remark about Kevin's shirt. Gloria, with lots of makeup on, brushed rudely by Tracy, jerking out her seat with disgust. Melinda was loudly telling anyone near her about the upcoming swim tournament she expected to win.

Already I regretted having agreed to teach this senior high summer school class, Personal Psychology. Half the kids didn't seem to want to be there. Many looked and acted as

BY BARBARA B. VARENHORST

if they didn't like themselves and didn't expect anyone else to like them either. It would be hard to tear down their defenses so that they would allow me to accept them, but I was determined. During our weeks together they were going to learn to value and respect something about themselves.

Think As Highly of Oneself As One Ought to Think

Adolescence is a time when young people search for the answer to "Who Am I?" As they do, they compare themselves to others, experiment, evaluate reactions of peers and adults, and try to sort out what this all means in terms of who they think they are. It is a time of enormous preoccupation with self, and if left to flounder in this morass of self-centeredness, kids often end up with a healthy case of self-hatred. Surveys indicate that 75 to 80 percent of teenagers say they struggle with self-hatred. Statistics on the incidence of teenage suicide, drug abuse, and sexual activity reveal the truth of these negative feelings about self.

How do we help youth combat self-hatred or prevent it from growing? How do we as Christians reconcile humility and dying to oneself with the idea of self-acceptance?

What *is* self-acceptance? Broadly defined, self-acceptance is a belief in oneself that includes a healthy valuing of one's good qualities and gifts and a realistic awareness and understanding of one's faults and limitations. Self-accepting people are not boastful or rude, nor do they display a "better than thou" attitude. On the contrary, true self-acceptance demands humility because you know you aren't perfect and you know you need forgiveness and help to overcome your weakness. But your litany of faults

must be overbalanced by the self-confidence and assurance of knowing that you are a child of God, and therefore a person of worth.

When young people are asked to list three things they dislike about themselves and three things they like, they have no trouble with the dislike list—in fact they don't stop at three items! But they often come up with a blank for the things they like, even when pressured to think of something. This is particularly true with Christian youth who see this as bragging and feel it is

> *Surveys indicate that 75 to 80 percent of teenagers say they struggle with self-hatred.*

wrong to brag. It *is* wrong to brag, but it is unchristian not to value oneself and the accomplishments that come with good stewardship of the talents and gifts God has given us. False humility—actually an effective way of getting attention—and running yourself down are insults to the Lord and a denial of ways in which we can honor Him.

Filling in the Missing Links

We tend not to realize a healthy appreciation for ourselves by merely thinking about it, talking about it,

or even contemplating how God loves us. As Tim Stafford says in his book, *Do You Sometimes Feel Like a Nobody?* (Campus Life Books), "People grow to accept themselves at about the same rate they climb outside themselves and actively care for others." It is significant that we don't automatically grow socially and emotionally just by getting older, as we do physically and mentally. Yet this is the type of growth and competence people need to climb outside themselves and know how to care for others. To be able to do this, to develop self-acceptance, young people need to help in learning the skills and developing the values that motivate them to do it.

Learning the Skills

A group of parents and students had gathered to discuss problems of adolescents. Parents talked of drugs, poor grades, and peer pressure. Then a nice-looking boy, speaking with hesitation, said, "I don't know how to make friends." Silence fell, and other students began nodding agreement. This boy had expressed the need many of them felt, which perhaps was why they had some of the problems the parents mentioned earlier.

This was the need of my students that summer, and much of what I taught them is described in my book *Real Friends* (Harper and Row, 1983). As they learned and practiced the skills of making friends, they began climbing out of themselves and actively caring for others.

Searching for ways to reach these young people, I assigned each student to observe a classmate for the remainder of the course, keeping the matching confidential so no one would know who was observing whom. Each was to watch the progress and growth of

> *Young people need a "permission push" to get them involved with others.*

the person assigned, and on the last day of class each would share observations. The task was intended not only to provide practice in "listening with your eyes," but to get students to focus on someone other than themselves. It worked—but unexpected things happened, too. When students knew they were being observed, their behavior improved. They became more positive and kind to one another. Their attitudes changed. They became more trusting and began opening up about their fears and insecurities.

The last day of class we went around the room, each having a turn at revealing whom he or she had observed and describing what had been seen. Each said wonderfully complimentary, helpful, and truthful things directly to the person who had earned them. It was an exciting and touching event to see the effect of positive affirmation from peers. I knew then my goal had been reached.

Promoting New Values

What also happened to my students was that they acquired new values. They came to see in classmates different qualities that over-

shadowed a shirt someone had on, a swimming trophy, a pimply face, or a scrawny body. Gradually they were letting go of the standards they had used to judge themselves and others.

It is difficult to penetrate the value system most young people use to gauge their worth. They see the values of looks, popularity, possessions, and good grades advertised and popularized. They compare themselves accordingly and often feel like losers. It isn't too surprising, then, how eagerly they respond to the discovery of new values that outrank in importance the ones they have been using.

Ask your young people to talk about someone besides their parents who has had a positive influence on their lives. Ask them to describe what it was about this person, what he or she did that made the difference, and why they remember this person. Start the process by talking about such a person in *your* life. When all have finished, have the group compile a list of the qualities, skills, or attitudes that made the difference in how they had been changed. Then ask them to measure themselves against this list and to acknowledge which of these qualities they feel

> *Self-hatred is healed by letting others love you so you can eventually love yourself.*

they have and which they would like. Then lead group members to talk about how they can help each other meet these goals.

In the many times I have done this exercise, never have I heard mentioned anything related to appearance, material gifts, or popularity. That fact has a powerful impact on those who participate. Out of their own lives they discover a new measure of their potential worth.

Providing the Courage To Grow

The skills and values you teach will never take root unless they are nourished through action. This requires help and a push to get young people involved in others' lives, as well as encouragement to trust themselves and others.

Young people need a "permission push" to get them involved with others so they can use the skills they have learned. Make it an assignment! Require that each of your youth has to find an *individual* project of helping or doing something for others. Give them some ideas, such as visiting an older person, tutoring a younger child, befriending a new student at school, etc. Let them brainstorm. Get them signed up. Review how they will proceed; supervise and help them as they do, encouraging them along the way so that each finds some success and satisfaction in what he or she is doing.

Allan, for example, said he had taken the class because he didn't like himself and didn't know how to make friends. When I got a request for someone to work with Kevin, a fifth-grade boy who had no friends and vented his need by picking fights, I thought of Allan. Allan was studious, nonathletic, and so gentle he probably never even *tried* to kill a fly. His eyes widened with fear when I asked him to help Kevin, and he gave me many reasons why he was not qualified. After I urged him to try by using his personality, thoughts, and skills, he reluctantly agreed. Gradually Kevin began to do less fighting. The two became good friends and eventually found the courage to reach out in friendship to their peers. Reflecting on the experience, Allan humbly admitted, "Kevin taught me to believe in myself and to like who I am."

Developing Trust

Self-hatred is healed by letting others love you so you can eventually love yourself. John Powell asked the question, "Why am I afraid to tell you who I am?" The answer he got was, "If I tell you who I am, you may not like who I am, and it's all that I have." Trust is being willing to tell another who you really are, anticipating respect and no negative judgment. Expres-

sion of feelings is the heart of telling another who you are. Young people find this hard to do, partly because they fear they will be judged negatively by others. Help them learn to express and trust.

Family conflict is a volatile topic to discuss in this way. Ask young people to talk about what a stranger might see or hear if he or she were to come to their homes at the dinner hour. Amazing things pour out, often heavily loaded with pain and hurt. It touches so many emotions that teenagers can forget about censoring words or "saying it just right," and feelings are expressed. Young people often react with quiet empathy, sometimes tears, hugs, or reaching for a hand to squeeze. Youth are respectful of sincerity and pain; these feelings choke the laughs and mocking, and release a flow of love. They free others to express feelings, too—and this is trust.

In the movie *The Breakfast Club*

one teenager asks another: "Why are you being so nice to me?"

The answer: "Because you are letting me." Trust is letting another like you, and when you do, you can begin liking yourself.

The only One you can fully trust is the Lord. But all those young people who struggle with self-hatred don't know this. They are spiritually deprived. This means our basic work in helping youth accept themselves with all their imperfections and uncertainties is to guide them in experiencing that trust. When they let the Lord not only like them, but love them, then they will be able to accept God's gift of who they are. □

Barbara B. Varenhorst, Ph.D., is director of the Palo Alto Peer Counseling Center in Palo Alto, California.

Jim Who?

About a coach who cared

When I entered Taylor University, where my brother Jim had been a track star several years earlier, I was extremely proud of his accomplishments. I also was determined to live up to his reputation. When track practice began in the spring, I was there working out with the rest of the guys. Built bigger and heavier than my brother, I realized I would never be the sprinter and long jumper Jim had been. I was better shaped for the shot put, javelin, and discus, so I worked on those three events.

But after three months of

practice, I wasn't making much progress. Discouraged, I went to see Coach Glass, a good friend of Jim's who had also become my friend. Sitting in the coach's office, I told him how discouraged I was, and how I felt I wouldn't ever be as good as Jim.

Suddenly the coach stopped me. Looking me in the eye, he asked, "Jim who?"

Coach Glass knew exactly who I was talking about. He also knew precisely what I was thinking and what I needed to hear. Those two short words had a

tremendous impact on the formation of my identity. I began to realize that I could never be Jim; I had to be Paul. And I had to be the best Paul I could be. That was how a caring coach helped me on the road to becoming the person I am today, and I'll never forget what he did for me.

—Paul Woods

Paul Woods *is an editor of youth publications at David C. Cook Publishing Co. He loves being an editor and writer, and is glad he is who he is.*

Test Flight to Adulthood

Sexuality helps to shape a teen's self-image— and fuels the flight to maturity.

Grant hung to the back of the line in the narthex. I was his new pastor, just out of seminary. At 16 he was a first-string back on the high school football team. He was beginning to get serious about Jesus when we came to town.

"Hey, Preach," he whispered, his eyes innocent and sparkling. "What do you think about girls?"

It was the first of several conversations in which he "gave me his questions," as he later described it. "See, I don't have anybody else I can give my questions to." That was in 1954.

B Y D O N A L D M. J O Y

Today, Grant is a grandfather, and his family has been special to us since we met him. He married the girl who first caught his attention back when he was 16.

More recently another 16-year-old, Bobby, began giving me *his* questions. One day he trapped me on my front porch and asked about masturbation. He wanted to know whether he was in danger of going to hell because of his sexual feelings, which were coming on so strong. Then he was feeling the crunch that comes when you have your first job and are offered drugs, pot, liquor, and sex—just for the asking. All he could do was shake his head and say, "I don't like the way I'm feeling. There's a part of me that wants to go out and get wasted tonight, just to see how it feels. And the guy who offered to take me out lives right over there." He pointed across the street from where we were sitting. A little more than two hours later, after a bowl of ice cream had gone down the hatch, I reached across the kitchen table to grab Bobby's hand and said, "Let's celebrate by giving it to God." We both prayed, and it was clear that he had taken a courageous step in being responsible for his life and his choices.

Grant and Bobby are separated by 1,000 miles and more than 30 years. But their innocent trust in me makes me take high school people and their sexuality very seriously.

The Test Flight

■

You are working with teens who will mature sexually at about 12 to 14. Yet they will have to keep that "treasure in earthen vessels" for about 10 years before presenting it as their gift on the wedding night.

Stone age children have it easy by comparison. They mature more slowly and have automatic social rites of passage which include fam-

ily presentations in marriage. But your kids, who live in a complicated culture with high technology, have to deal with very complicated moral questions including nuclear energy, economics, and medicine—as well as sexuality.

Sexual energy is the fuel which fires the adolescent years. And when one looks across cultures, it is clear that the suffering which sexual energy brings is God's unique curriculum for bringing insight and wisdom within reach of every person at a level appropriate to his or her culture.

Pubescence is a period of about two years during which the developing human body is changed from a childhood body to an adult body. Pubescence ushers in basic changes in body chemistry and shape, and is most evident in the profound changes in the sex system. Both females and males develop hair which serves as a marker of body maturity. Hair on armpit and groin for both sexes, and facial hair for males fulfills the literal meaning of the word *pubescence:* "to become hairy." When a girl has her first period or a boy experiences first ejaculation, both know the personal meaning of pubescence.

Along with the changes in the main lines of a person's body, there is a period of about six years during which the brain continues to experience this assault of hormonal chemicals. An adolescent's sex system is literally saturating the whole body with massive doses of hormones. Growth spurts and acne are likely effects.

Mood shifts are common when hormones hit the brain. But as the body ripens, so do the emotions. Unfortunately, many kids deal with these mood shifts by retreating, getting depressed, or getting drunk. It is a pity to mask the adult maturing experience with drugs or alcohol when emotions are doing the yo-yo. Many teens who get into

such masks for their feelings remain addicted throughout life and never know the peace of being fully alive and fully human. They never discover the "high" of simply being alive and well, but instead live all day for the cocktail hour or the six-pack to space them out every evening.

Through all these changes a wonderful thing is happening deep inside the brain. The brain is developing a new capacity. Most childhood decisions are made because children learn to tell right from wrong. But adult life is more complicated, and it often tosses questions in your lap for which there are no easy answers. Adults need a "reasoning machine" that can walk around a problem or a question and speculate at the consequences of several different choices. This process is called "reversible reasoning," and it goes on deep inside the brain in the correlation fibers of the central cortex. That part of the brain remains "green" and insulated with myelin sheathing until about four to six years after puberty. This means that an adolescent may have the body of an adult, but still be stuck with a child's brain for a few years.

One of the first signs of this maturing brain shows up when the teen locks the bathroom door and doesn't come out for a long time. The mirror hears it all: "Am I ever going to look decent? Will anybody think I am pretty/handsome? Will anyone love me just for who I am? What I would give to know I'm not going to be a giraffe, hippopotamus, or orangutan! Why would God ever make anybody like me? What does He want from me?"

When teens have to make choices about drugs and sex before their reversible reasoning is working well, they need the support of some clear rules to live by. But in a few years they'll be able to turn a few principles into specific answers to adult questions. Jesus said two principles would handle every question: Love God with your entire being, and love your neighbor as you love yourself (Mark 12:30,31).

As I told one young friend, Dan, "The response Jesus wants from you is to love Him with all your mind, soul, and strength, and that means your entire self—your new and complete sexual self. Your fertility, God's personal gift of creativity handed to you, is yours. But Jesus asks you to give it back so He can sanctify it and let you really live, lifelong, with the natural high of honesty as you walk in obedience to Him, and maintain integrity in all of your relationships."

The Test Pilots

So look at your youth as "test pilots" who are going through the moral stresses which will push them to the higher realm of moral, ethical, and spiritual insight they so much need. Their sexuality is the aircraft in which they are propelled. In their sexuality they are tested on honesty, valuing other people, and making decisions that matter most to generations yet unborn.

Some people explode in flames simply because they want everything they can get, and they want it now. Others have to make an emergency landing for repairs because one or two bad decisions brought them down. But all of them suffer a little every day the test flight is their agenda. They are making good choices, but their sexual energy feels like it is going to explode, now!

It is amazing but true that those who make emergency landings because of a poor choice, *and* those who survive the stresses of the moral sound barrier in mid-flight, can make it to sensitive Christian maturity. Both have suffered enough that Jesus can use their pain to turn them loose as leaders and healers.

We should especially applaud those who have made the tough and good choices and landed safe, though stressed, in adulthood. If they can reflect honestly on the pain of abstinence and the joy of integrity, they will make our finest graduates into the adult ranks.

As your young people make their test flights into adulthood, you can be their "flight instructor." Their performance can become both their risk and yours. If kids trust you with the truth it will be because they know you are "safe." If you pushed them they would tell you, as one young man told me before unloading a heavy problem, "I don't know why, but from watching you I think you can help me."

The teen test flight, fueled by sexuality, can be a rough one. But if you have honestly faced your own journey and received God's forgiveness and healing, your experience can be transformed into a credential for listening to the current generation of test pilots. □

Donald M. Joy, Ph.D., is professor of human development and Christian education at Asbury Theological Seminary. He is the author of Bonding: Relationships in the Image of God *(1985) and* Rebonding: Preventing and Restoring Damaged Relationships *(1986), both published by Word.*

Talking to Teens About Sexual Identity

Author Tim Stafford offers these thoughts for teens who worry about being "real men" and "real women":

God made you what you are. He did not make you in the image of Miss America or Bill Cosby or anybody else. He made you to reflect His character as the unique character you are. You do not, therefore, have to worry that He left out some crucial ingredient. You do not have to feel concern that one of your chromosomes may be missing.

The only ideal male or female to measure yourself against is yourself—you as God wants you to be.

God has a wonderful destiny for you. It isn't as though you are a finished product. God made you what you are, but more importantly He wants to make you what you need to be. His plan doesn't just include your "spiritual" nature. It includes your sexual nature. God offers unlimited potential to anyone willing to follow Him.

The difference between girls and boys is really not that important. "In Christ," Paul wrote, "there is no male or female." He didn't mean that male and female are identical. He meant that in the really important things of life, sexuality isn't even a category. Whether you are a "real man" or a "real woman" doesn't affect your life in Jesus Christ.

Reprinted by permission from Campus Life *magazine,* Christianity Today, Inc. © 1985.

Hope for Marginal Kids in the Puberty Rush

Q: What do you say or do to encourage the teen who, when everybody else grows up, is still trapped in a little kid's body?

A: Everybody has a personal calendar or clock that dictates when major growth will occur and when it will stop. I've sometimes told parent groups to watch for tips that growth is complete; most girls are within one inch of adult height when they have their first menstrual period, for example. Boys are usually growing until they produce stiff-bristle whiskers which need daily shaving. Here are other clues:

Heredity. Suggest that kids study family photographs, taking into account how old the relatives were when the pictures were made. This can tell kids whether they're from a tribe of fast or slow maturers. Were relatives tall, fat, skinny, or short? In recent centuries, children have tended to be a little taller (and a lot better looking) than their parents. Kids are more likely to be genuine look-alikes of their grandparents—at their age—than of their parents.

Feet. Help kids to appreciate personal body characteristics. Size of foot is a good predictor of height. A 12-year-old boy, for example, may not yet have hit a major growth spurt, but he may have a shoe size about the same as his father's.

Q: But what do you say to the teen who knows he or she isn't pretty or handsome—the kid with the birthmark indelibly printed across the face, or with the conspicuous deformity or injury? What can you say to the young person who has a progressively disabling disease, or is dwarfed in some irreversible way?

A: These have to be the toughest cases of all. But they also have in them the stuff from which greatness is made. I suspect that people who rely on their good looks and handsome bodies tend to be lazier than the rest of us. And those of us who carry deformity or other handicapping conditions, including broken noses and ears that point the wrong way, are spared the competition for "most beautiful person of the year." Instead, we can concentrate on being honest and gentle with people who do come close enough to get to know us. We can develop skills we do have until we excel in a few gifts which serve other people. These gifts then become our "faces" and our "bodies." And people who get to know us for whom we really are don't pay much attention to the physical package in which we live.

Tell kids what comes to mind as you look through your old high school yearbook. Tell them about sports kings and queens who by middle age no longer have beautiful bodies. Urge them to keep their eyes open as they return to their own reunions across the decades. They should watch the eyes of others; people with good character keep showing it in their eyes and their faces. Your kids may be surprised to see that some of the good-lookers never developed a sense of integrity. Chances are that few of the handsome ones will have developed the beautiful spirit of service and friendship that others must cultivate just to make it anywhere with anybody. Those who have cultivated that spirit will be the winners.

—Donald Joy

Aim

Overview

You'll Need

Myself in the Mirror

To help kids understand that God knows everything about them, yet loves them anyway. Key passage: Psalm 139.

We all feel insecure and uneasy about certain things. In a way, even thoughts of God can make us feel more insecure; we may assume that because He is so perfect, He couldn't understand mistakes and weaknesses. This meeting is designed to show kids an exciting side of God which should help them to accept themselves.

1. Our View of Others (Brainstorming) 10-15 min.
   - □ Chalkboard or overhead projector

2. Our View of Ourselves (Eulogy writing) 15-20 min.
   - □ My Eulogy (activity piece A1 from the back of this book)
   - □ pencils
   - □ prescription pill bottle
   - □ slips of paper

3. God's View of Us (Bible study) 10-15 min.
   - □ Bibles

4. Our View of God (Response and prayer) 10 min.
   - □ matches and aluminum pie pan

BY FRED HARTLEY

Discovering that we all play the "critic" game. Standing next to the overhead projector or chalkboard, pop the question: **When you meet a new kid, what basis do you use to form an opinion? With what standards do we judge others?** (Clothes, hairstyle, smell of one's breath, complexion, etc.) Write answers on the transparency or board. Try to get everyone to participate; 25 to 30 different answers should not be difficult in a large group.

Next, ask the *guys* this question: **Who do you think is the prettiest girl in the world?** (Wait for a few good answers.) **What is it about this girl that appeals to you?** Try to determine the basis of their value judgments.

Then give the *girls* equal time: **Who do you think is the most handsome, attractive guy in the world? What attracts you to this person?**

After drawing out answers and determining the basis of the girls' value judgments, look at the negative side: **What are some nicknames you've used or heard used for kids who have something "wrong" with them? Go all the way back to kindergarten if you have to.** If kids come up dry, get more specific by asking for names used to describe those with. . .

- *Personality* problems (weirdo, turkey, hot dog, jerk, nerd).
- *Intellectual* problems (fool, airhead, space cadet, fuzzball, mastodon).
- *Physical* problems (dog, blimp, crater face, tinsel teeth, scab).
- *Agility* problems (spaz, klutz).
- *Moral* problems (slut, playboy, creep).

Finally, ask: **How does it feel to have one of these names used against you?** (Allow kids to discuss their feelings if they feel free to do so.)

Identifying the way we see ourselves, and the way we think others see us.

It's interesting that we often use the same standards to judge ourselves that we use to judge others. Let's have some fun right now with the way we see ourselves—and the way we think others see us. Pass out copies of "My Eulogy" (activity piece A1). You can expect reactions like, "Oh, gross!" and "How morbid!" Explain: **This is to be filled out as honestly as possible and read by your best friend at a memorial service for you in front of the entire student body at your school.** Encourage kids to complete at least half the sentences. After four minutes, have a few kids read theirs. Try to select some readers whose answers are likely

1. Our View Of Others

(Discussion) 10-15 min.

2. Our View Of Ourselves

(Eulogy writing) 15-20 min.

to be serious as well as some who will be silly or hilarious. Discuss how it felt to write the eulogies; was it hard or easy for kids to come up with positive things about themselves?

Next, pull a prescription pill bottle from your pocket and ask: **If you could take a pill, knowing that pill would change one thing about yourself, what would you want that thing to be? It could be your parents, home situation, looks, height, abilities, brains, coordination, whatever. Don't say it out loud, but think of it.**

Now, out of the pill bottle, pull small slips of paper to be handed to everyone present. Without allowing anyone else to see, each person should write on the slip of paper the thing he or she would like changed—and then fold up the paper as small as possible. Have kids hold onto these folded-up papers until the end of the meeting.

---

3. God's View of Us

(Bible study) 10-15 min.

Discovering how well God knows us. Read Psalm 139, calling on a good reader or reading randomly without putting any poor reader on the spot. Ask: **According to this, what does God know about us?** (Where we live, where we go to school, what we say, our parents, our appearance, our reputation, etc.)

How does the way we see others and ourselves differ from the way God sees us? Is there anything we can keep from God, anywhere we can go to get away from Him? (No.)

What do you think God is most concerned about when it comes to you and me?

Now, the big question: Of the things you'd like to change about yourself, which are unchangeable—determined by God? (Height, basic facial appearance, basic abilities, etc.) **What things about ourselves are changeable?** (Posture, complexion, study habits, attitudes, etc.)

---

4. Our View Of God

(Response and prayer) 10 min.

Realizing that God knew what He was doing in making us as He did, and that He loves us even though He knows us so well. Using Psalm 139, explain that God is all-knowing or omniscient (vss. 1-6); all-present or omnipresent (vss. 7-12); all-powerful or omnipotent (vss. 13-18); and holy (vss. 19-24). **He could have made us taller or shorter or with a different facial structure. He could have given us different parents or even had us born into a different race in a whole different country. But for some reason the God who knows everything about us and who could have made us different chose to create us exactly the** way He did. He loves us just the way we are (John 3:16; I John 3:1; 4:19).

Remember that little piece of paper you folded up? Remember that area you would change if you had the power? If that area is changeable, it's up to you to change it. If it's unchangeable, it's up to you to accept it.

Collect the folded-up pieces of paper in an aluminum pie pan. Strike a match and set fire to the papers. **Some of us carry around in our minds a list of things we wish we could change about ourselves—but can't. We keep looking at that list and thinking we're not worth as much as the next person—who probably has a list, too. We don't have to do that. We can let those things go—even thank God for them because they're part of what makes us unique.** Lead the group in a simple prayer: **"Lord Jesus, thank You for making me just the way I am. Thank You for knowing everything about me, and loving me. Thank You even for . . ."** Have kids silently fill in the blank with the traits or situations they wrote on their slips of paper.

Fred Hartley *is pastor of the South Dade Alliance Church in Leisure City, Florida. His books for young people include* Flops *(Fleming Revell, 1985), about failure and self-image.*

Aim

Overview

You'll Need

As Seen on TV!

To help kids identify how advertising has influenced the way they see themselves, and, as needed, to counteract that influence with God's view. Key passage: Matthew 5:1-12.

Your teens are prime targets of the most sophisticated, well-bankrolled persuasion machine in history: modern advertising. Unfortunately, many ads exploit a kid's search for identity, implying that to be without a certain product is to be incomplete or inferior. And the "ideal" teen image presented in ads is often anything but Biblical. This session will help your kids decide which of their assumptions about themselves come from Madison Avenue, and which come from Scripture.

1. Commercial Chaos (Mini-party) 15-20 min.
   - □ a costume
   - □ videotape player and TV or audio cassette player (with recorded commercials)
   - □ teen magazines
   - □ prizes
   - □ refreshments

2. The Selling of Sludge (Skit) 5-10 min.
   - □ The Selling of Sludge (Activity piece B1)
   - □ three volunteer actors

3. Process of Elimination (Self-test) 5-10 min.

4. Says Who? (Bible study) 10-15 min.
   - □ Says Who? (Activity piece B2)
   - □ pens or pencils
   - □ Bibles

5. Be-Ad-Itudes (Creating commercials) 10-15 min.

BY JOHN DUCKWORTH

*R*ealizing that advertising has a big, sometimes surprising, influence on all of us. At least a week before the meeting, inform kids that they're to dress up for this occasion—as characters from TV commercials (Ronald McDonald, Max Headroom, Doublemint twins, a local car dealer, various celebrity endorsers, etc.). If possible, have them arrive early to allow extra time for fun. Create a party atmosphere, even serving refreshments (like chips and bubble gum) commonly pitched to kids via TV. For extra ambience, decorate the room with ads from teen magazines.

In the background, play a video or audio tape on which you've recorded nothing but commercials. As soon as the party's underway, stage one or more of the following contests to determine your group's "advertising I.Q.":

1. *Name That Product.* Display a selection of slogans and logos you've cut from magazines; see who can name the products or companies behind them.

2. *Jingle Singing.* Break the group into trios or quartets and find out who can provide the best rendition of a currently popular TV commercial jingle.

3. *The Big Finish.* Using your prerecorded video or audio tape, play just the first few seconds of several commercials and see who can act out or describe the unplayed portions.

Award prizes (preferably something advertised on TV) to the winners. Then give out prizes for the most original, most elaborate, and hardest-to-identify commercial character costumes. Wrap up the mini-party by noting how familiar most of us are with advertisements. That's because they tend to stick in our minds—even when we think we haven't paid attention to them.

*S*eeing that ads don't always have our best interests at heart. Have three of your best readers perform the skit, "The Selling of Sludge" (activity piece B1). It's a good idea to have rehearsed at least once during the week; encourage your actors to ham it up and to read loudly and clearly. Be sure to introduce the characters and situation. Afterward, discuss the skit along these lines:

■ **What were Blubwell and Fleem really interested in?**

■ **What did they want their advertising to do?**

■ **How did they hope to appeal to teenagers? How do the ads you see and hear try to appeal to you?**

■ **Do you think the teenagers in Sludge commercials will be beautiful and handsome—or plain? Will they wear current styles or outdated ones? Have clear skin or blemishes? Ride dune buggies or read books? What other traits will**

1. Commercial Chaos

(Mini-party)
10-15 min.

2. The Selling of Sludge

(Skit)
5-10 min.

3. Process of Elimination

(Self-test)
5-10 min.

4. Says Who?

(Bible study)
10-15 min.

they probably have—or seem to have?

Point out that, unlike the characters in the skit, many advertisers are not intentionally dishonest. But many ads imply that it's important to look, dress, and act in a particular way—and that using a product is part of that acceptable look and behavior. The truth is that drinking all that pop, wearing all those clothes, and using all those cosmetics won't make us "okay" like the people in the ads.

*I*dentifying ways in which advertising can warp the way we see ourselves. Ask: **Do you measure up to advertising's image of the "right" kind of teenager?** Read the following "eliminators." Pause after each one to give kids time to think about whether or not they measure up:

■ **You have plenty of money to spend on albums, clothes, and concerts.**

■ **If you're a girl, you're as slender as the girls in the jeans commercials.**

■ **If you're a guy, you're muscular and good at sports.**

■ **You have a perfect complexion.**

■ **You never do anything embarrassing around other people.**

■ **You have a boyfriend or girlfriend.**

■ **Others think you're sexy.**

■ **You're usually happy and having fun.**

■ **You don't spend much time with parents, and you're never seen in church.**

■ **You know and wear the latest fashions and hairstyles.**

Ask how many of your kids match these "ideal" images (no one will in every respect). Point out that advertising directed at *adults* can affect teens, too, by holding out an ideal adult image to grow into. Ask: **What are "ideal" adults in ads like?** (Usually sophisticated, having plenty of money and nice clothes and houses and cars, attractive to the opposite sex, surrounded by friends or family, happy, etc.) **How does it feel to fall short of people who are featured in ads, especially when we see them so often?** (If your kids won't reveal their feelings, talk about how others at school might be affected.)

*F*inding out how God's "ideal" for us differs from the one(s) presented in most advertising. Have your kids fill out "Says Who?" (activity piece B2) individually or in teams. Then discuss the results, which may vary widely. Explain that "poor in spirit" (vs. 3) can be taken to mean those who realize their spiritual poverty, their need for God, as well as those who lack money. Verses which could be applied to the ad-type statements include these: (A) vs. 4; (B) vss. 10,11; (C) vs. 8; (D) vs. 7; (E) vss. 3, 5; (F) all; (G) vs. 5; (H) vs. 7, 9; (I) vss. 6, 10, 11; (J) vss. 3, 6. Read these verses aloud and help kids make the connections.

Ask: **How was Jesus Himself an example of these traits?** Point out that Jesus' way to real happiness is based on the fact that the Christian life lasts forever. Our rewards are in Heaven, not necessarily here. Most advertising emphasizes "rewards" (many of them unattainable) which don't last long.

*S*ubstituting God's values for those contained in most advertising. Break the group into small "ad agencies" whose job is to "sell" the values of the Beatitudes (Matthew 5:1-12). Assign each agency to come up with a 20-second commercial for one of the "blesseds." Each commercial should emphasize (without exaggerating) the benefits of that trait—for example, inheriting the earth as a benefit of meekness. Encourage kids to use their own words (to explain phrases such as "poor in spirit" and "be filled"), and to be as creative and persuasive as possible. When the commercials are ready, have participants act them out.

Close the session by challenging kids to take advertising messages with a grain of "salt" (Matthew 5:13-16). Then pray, thanking God that He loves and accepts us, and that He has provided ways for us to be truly happy—even if those ways aren't "seen on TV."

John Duckworth *is editor of church resources at the David C. Cook Publishing Co. He has worked with youth and has written books, articles, stories, and plays.*

5. Be-Ad-Itudes

(Creating commercials)
10-15 min.

Aim

Overview

You'll Need

Finding Yourself Without Being Selfish

To help kids avoid destructive rebellion against parents and harmful conformity to peers as they discover their own identities. Key passage: Galatians 5:13.

Breaking away from parents and peers is an important part of discovering one's identity. As teens grow, they experience increasing freedom from parental restrictions—along with substantial peer pressure. Kids without a strong sense of identity often choose behaviors which are irresponsible, self-destructive, and hurtful to others. This session will help kids see that they tend to choose behaviors which are consistent with the way they see themselves. It will also encourage them to use their growing freedom responsibly by choosing behaviors which serve God and others.

1. The Dil Phonahue Show (Panel discussion) 20-25 min.
   - ☐ panel of five or six youth
   - ☐ preliminary meeting with your panel
   - ☐ costumes, microphone (optional)

2. Who Do People Say That I Am? (Bible study I) 10-15 min.
   - ☐ Bibles
   - ☐ pencils
   - ☐ Under Pressure? (activity piece C1)

3. Loving Freedom (Bible study II) 10-15 min.

4. Freedom Commitment (Response) 5 min.
   - ☐ Freedom Commitment (activity piece C2)

BY STEVE PETERSON

Meeting C

Exploring the relationship between freedom and responsibility. During the week before the meeting, select a group of young people to play roles on your panel. The roles should reflect various perspectives on the issue of freedom vs. responsibility. Some suggestions: a set of parents, a teenage punker, a pastor, a politician, a hedonist, a teenager committed to Christ. Feel free to use others. Kids should dress their roles and try to respond as the people they're representing would, not as they themselves would. Encourage kids to really get into their roles.

As leader, you play and dress the part of Dil Phonahue. Get things rolling by asking the panel a few questions. When the discussion gets going you can take questions from the audience (played by the rest of your youth group). Kids may address questions to a panel member, or you may go down the line and ask each panelist to respond to the question. Encourage panelists to respond to each other's answers. Initial questions might include:

■ **What do you feel individual freedom is?**

■ **Based on your own definition, in what ways are you free?**

■ **What are some ways in which you are not free?**

■ **Do you feel some people lose the freedom to be themselves by caving in to peer pressure? What are some examples?**

Come up with other questions based on kids' answers. You should be able to demonstrate that freedom is desirable, but freedom without responsibility leads to disorder, self-destruction, and harm to others.

1. The Dil Phonahue Show

(Panel discussion)
20-25 min.

Examining Jesus' understanding of Himself. Assure your kids that feeling pressure to compromise their identities in order to satisfy someone else's expectations isn't new or limited to them. People even had wrong expectations of Jesus.

Have your kids read Luke 9:18, 19. In this passage Jesus asks, "Who do the crowds say I am?" Point out that even though the disciples had a number of different responses to His question, Jesus did not compromise who He was in order to live up to others' expectations.

Have kids read John 6:15.

■ **How did Jesus respond to the people's pressure on Him to become an earthly king?**

■ **If a multitude were pressuring you to become their leader, but you knew it wasn't right for you, could you resist?**

■ **Do you ever feel pressured to do something you know**

2. Who Do People Say That I Am?

(Bible study I)
10-15 min.

isn't right in order to gain the recognition of your friends?

Jesus knew who He was—and whose He was—and that gave Him strength to resist doing things that were not God's will. Pass out copies of ''Under Pressure?'' (activity piece C2). Have kids answer the questions and write down their completions of the sentence starters; then discuss their answers in small groups or with the whole group.

As you wrap up this section of the meeting, ask: **How can knowing that you are God's child help you resist peer pressure?** (Allow time for kids to answer.)

3. Loving Freedom

(Bible study II) 10-15 min.

Discovering the need for restrictions. Say: **God doesn't offer His children a life of rules and restrictions, but a life of freedom. God wants us, however, to use our freedom to glorify Him and serve others, not to serve our selfish desires.**

Have kids read Luke 15:11-24. Point out that the father gave the son freedom to choose how and for whom he would live. Discuss the following questions:

■ **How did the Prodigal Son use his freedom?**

■ **What happened to him when he used it to serve his own selfish desires?**

■ **What are some ways that people abuse or misuse the freedom God gives us today?**

■ **What are some things that could happen to us today if we abuse or misuse the freedom God has given us?**

■ **How might the son's journey have been an attempt to find his own identity?**

■ **How do kids today sometimes attempt to discover who they are?**

Have kids turn to Galatians 5:13 and read it to themselves. Then read it aloud and discuss its meaning. Ask: **According to this passage, what is the key to practicing the freedom we have in Christ?** Wait for answers. Note that abundant life and complete identity are found in relationship to Christ as we love and serve others in Him. Jesus said, ''Whoever wants to save his life will lose it, but whoever loses his life for me will save it'' (Luke 9:24). When the Prodigal Son gave up trying to serve himself and returned to his father, he discovered new life.

4. Freedom Commitment

(Response) 5 min.

Agreeing to use our freedom according to God's principles. Pass out copies of ''Freedom Commitment'' (activity piece C2). This exercise will give your young people a chance to process what this meeting means to them and to respond to that personal meaning. Responses may be discussed in the group, or you may want to let kids keep their answers to themselves. Let teens know before they write their answers whether you are going to ask them to share what they write.

In the "My Prayer" section of the sheet, have kids write brief, personal prayers in response to what you have talked about during this meeting. Now might be a good time to challenge those who have not made a commitment to Christ to do so. Close the meeting by letting students silently lift their prayers to God; then pray audibly yourself.

Steve Peterson *is youth pastor at Our Saviour's Reformed Church in Lakewood, Colorado. He's been working with young people for nearly a decade.*

Aim

Overview

You'll Need

Understanding and Accepting Your Sexual Identity

To help kids grasp God's will and purpose in creating them as sexual beings, and to enhance their self-esteem as males and females. Key passage: Genesis 1:27.

Today some people consider it unsophisticated or sexist to glorify—or even feel good about—being male or female. But there *is* significance and meaning in being a man or woman. Since teens are bombarded with androgynous models, especially in the music scene, it is important that they hear and understand the Lord's plan of mutuality, dependence, and balance between the sexes.

1. If We Were God (Imagination exercise) 10-15 min.
   - □ pencils
   - □ paper

2. Without You I'm Nothing (Demonstration) 10 min.

3. How 'Not Good' Became 'Good' (Bible study) 15-20 min.
   - □ Bibles
   - □ How It All Got Started (activity piece D1)
   - □ pencils

4. One Plus One Equals One (Object lesson and wrap-up) 10-15 min.
   - □ yellow and blue watercolors or poster paints
   - □ two one-inch paintbrushes
   - □ white poster board

BY MARY ANN MAYO

Realizing that God's choice to create two sexes is part of a grand plan. Divide into small groups. Pass out pencils and paper to each group. Ask kids to write how they might have created people if they were God. What height, weight, features, and abilities might people have? How many noses? How many ears? Get students' imaginations rolling by giving a couple of examples of how *you* might have made people if you'd had a choice. Explain that God could have done anything He wanted. Reproduction could have been by cloning, or through new creations. Companionship needs could have been met through a ''best buddy'' for Adam rather than through Eve.

After a few minutes, ask each group to share its alternative creation plans. Have fun with the answers, noting creativity, but point out that God didn't choose to do any of those things even though He could have. In His sovereignty, He chose to make two sexes.

■ **What is the most important result of having been made two sexes?**

There are many answers to this, but they all can be reduced to the fact that God intends that we relate as men and women. God is the author of sex and sexual relationships.

■ **Since relating as men and women can sometimes get us into trouble and cause us to break God's Law, why didn't God make a switch to turn off our sexual natures until marriage?**

Encourage kids to keep using their imaginations as they respond. Then introduce the concept that God intended people—married or single—to relate to each other as men and women, boys and girls, not asexual blobs. God has given us guidelines and the ability to keep our relationships on a plane that glorifies Him. This is not to be done by pretending sexual identity—our identity as a female or male—doesn't exist.

Demonstrating interdependence, trust, and vulnerability, the basis of male/female relationships. **God made two sexes and expects us to interact with one another as the man or woman we happen to be. Our relationship involves interdependence (we need each other), trust, and vulnerability. Let's demonstrate what it means.**

Have kids stand and pair off, one girl with each guy. Take turns if there's an uneven mix. Don't worry about differences in height as the pairs do the following two exercises; the more divergent the physical types, the more the point is made.

1. If We Were God

(Imagination exercise) 10-15 min.

2. Without You I'm Nothing

(Demonstration) 10 min.

1. Lean on one another back to back; each person is to move his or her feet forward until both depend on the other to remain upright.

2. Stand facing one another; put hands together over heads at a 45-degree angle, stepping back until balance is dependent on the cooperation of each participant.

After all pairs have done both exercises, ask: **What things are necessary to make these exercises work? Did size make a difference?**

Each team member brought his or her unique characteristics to this demonstration. In order to remain upright each male and female had to work out a distinctive balance. Let's see what the Bible has to say about this.

3. How 'Not Good' Became 'Good'

(Bible study) 15-20 min.

*E*xamining the revelation of God's plan for sexual identity. Divide again into mixed-sex small groups. Hand out "How It All Got Started" (activity piece D1). Read aloud Genesis 1:27, 28, 31 and 2:18-25. Have kids fill out the quiz (explaining that some answers rely on opinion as well as on the passage) and discuss it along these lines:

■ **Tell why you agree or disagree with each statement (or the attitude expressed by the statement). Support your opinion from the Bible passage.**

■ **Ask the other groups your own humorous question from the passage.**

■ **Share an idea about God's plan for you as a male or female that perhaps you hadn't given much thought to before.**

■ **How is what Genesis says different from society's message?**

■ **How is God's message about the purpose of our sexuality distorted in certain areas of the music scene? How could blurring the line between male and female affect the way kids feel about themselves? When women and men are portrayed *only* as sexual beings, how might that affect the way kids see themselves and others?**

4. One Plus One Equals One

(Object lesson and wrap-up) 15 min.

*R*einforcing the concept of God's purpose in creating two sexes. Take poster paint or watercolor, and on a large piece of white paper, paint a bold line, figure, or X in blue. Explain that it would be hard to describe blue if it were the only color in the world—other than saying that it contrasted with the paper. Then paint a similar figure, line, or X in yellow. Point out that now a distinction can be made.

Blue can be defined as it differs from yellow. Each color gives dimension and definition to the other. Now paint a figure, line, or X using *both* colors. The result is a third color, green.

God's intent was not for us to ignore who we are as male or female, nor for one sex to "lord" it over the other. God's plan is for us to relate to others in the fullness of who we are as male or female. Each of us is beautiful and distinct as we are, but something equally beautiful occurs when we relate fully and honestly with one another. It's almost as if a new color is created. This is especially true of the most intimate of human relationships—marriage. The partners do not cease being individuals, but their relationship takes on an identity of its own. The Bible calls this being "one flesh."

■ **How might this discussion change the way you feel about your sex or the opposite sex?**

Close the meeting with a prayer that gives thanks for God's majesty and wisdom in making two sexes, each with so much to offer the other. Ask for wisdom in relating to the opposite sex with understanding and acceptance.

Mary Ann Mayo *is a marriage and family counselor in Redlands, California. She is the author of* A Parent's Guide to Sex Education.

Aim

Overview

You'll Need

Learning to Live With Yourself

To help kids get along with themselves over the long haul, preparing them for the ups and downs their self-esteem is likely to encounter. Key passages: Philippians 1:3-11; 3:12-16.

No matter how hard teens work to find and accept themselves, they will still have some traits they don't like—or that others reject. Learning to live with limitations, yet growing, is a step of Christian maturity. This session will help your teens see that perfection won't come until they get to Heaven—and that God can begin to change them in the meantime.

---

1. Maniacal Makeovers (Contest) 5 min.
   - □ four volunteers
   - □ lots of cosmetics, two hairbrushes
   - □ two old bed sheets or other large cloths
   - □ table

2. Not Finished Yet (Dream list) 10-15 min.
   - □ Please Be Patient (activity piece E1 from the back of this book)
   - □ pencils

3. The Work Goes On (Bible study) 15-20 min.
   - □ paper
   - □ pencils
   - □ Bibles

4. Ripening Fruit (Self-evaluation) 10-15 min.
   - □ Progress Report (activity piece E2)
   - □ pencils

BY SANDY LARSEN

Realizing that we can't always change ourselves—or be changed—as quickly as we might like. You'll need four volunteers for this one—two "beauty experts" and two "victims." It's a good idea to talk with the victims before the meeting to make sure they wear grubbies and are *very* good sports. Use your own judgment in choosing guys or girls; a mixture would probably yield the funniest results.

Bring a selection of cosmetics, a couple of hairbrushes, and plenty of cold cream or other makeup remover, and put them on a table in front. Seat the victims at the table and announce that you're going to do a couple of beauty makeovers like they do in the women's magazines. The catch is that the makeovers must be completed in two minutes, and the winner will be the victim who ends up looking *least* like himself or herself. Use old bed sheets or other cloths to cover the victims' clothing, give the signal, and set the beauty experts to work. Call time in two minutes and have the group select the winner. You might want to take a photo of the results.

As the victims remove their makeup, discuss what happens when we try to change ourselves too quickly—we make mistakes. It takes time to change, and sometimes we need *real* expert help. When it comes to changing people, God is the Ultimate Expert.

Identifying our long-term goals for change. Hand out pencils and copies of "Please Be Patient" (activity piece E1). Read the quote from the woman in her 80s and tell kids to complete the "dream list" for themselves.

Kids will probably scribble a few ambitions, then run out of ideas. Don't be afraid if they stop writing for a while; give them time to ponder, and their pencils will start moving again.

Invite kids to share their dream lists if they wish; they can share selected parts if some dreams are too personal. Discourage any snickering at others' dreams, reminding kids that most great ideas sound a little crazy at first! **You have a lot of dreams and ambitions for the future, and that means you expect God to do a lot more with you than He has so far. I have things I'd like to do and be, too, before I reach 100.** Read your own dream list; it will help kids see that God is still at work on adults, too. **If we're Christians, we have plenty of time for God to make things happen in our lives—forever, in fact. So let's not be too hard on ourselves if we're not yet all He wants us to be. We're going to look at what Scripture says about living with our unfinished, imperfect selves.**

1. Maniacal Makeovers

(Contest) 5 min.

2. Not Finished Yet

(Dream list) 10-15 min.

3. The Work Goes On

(Bible study) 15-20 min.

Observing Paul's attitude toward the uncompleted process of perfection in others and himself. Have students get into pairs or threes. Hand out paper. Give the following instructions:

Group 1: Read Philippians 1:3-11 and write as many phrases as you can that describe the *character* of the Philippian Christians.

Group 2: Read Philippians 1:3-11 and write Paul's *hopes* for the Philippian Christians.

Group 3: Read Philippians 1:3-11 and describe the kind of people Paul wanted the Philippian Christians to *become.*

Group 4: Read Philippians 3:12-16 and describe Paul's attitude toward his *past.*

Group 5: Read Philippians 3:12-16 and describe Paul's attitude toward his *future.*

If you have more than five small groups, give duplicate instructions to some of them. As they work, move among them to offer help and encouragement. Then call time and ask groups to report what they have discovered from the Scriptures. Use the following summary as needed.

The character of the Philippian Christians: They had shared in Paul's preaching and sympathized with him in his imprisonment; they showed genuine concern for the man who had led them to Christ. We might look at them and think they had "arrived" spiritually.

Paul's hopes for the Philippian Christians: Despite the Philippians' good character, Paul looked forward to their further growth. He hoped for increasing love, knowledge, and righteousness in them. Yet he knew that the process would not be complete until Christ returned (or until they died and went to be with Christ). Emphasize verse 6—it is the Lord who began this good work, and it is the Lord who continues it and will continue it. That was true for the Philippians; it's true for us.

The kind of people Paul wanted the Philippian Christians to become: more loving, more knowledgeable, more discerning, approving what is excellent, pure, blameless, full of the results of righteousness. They still had a lot of growing to do, even though they had already reached a level of maturity. They were in good shape spiritually, but needed to go on.

Paul's attitude toward his future: He was "pressing on toward the goal." What lay ahead of him was a deeper maturing in the Lord, and ultimate perfection in Heaven. His mind and will were directed toward that goal. In one sense he liked where he was spiritually; in another sense he intended not to stay there.

Ask: **Based on these verses, what might Paul tell us when we feel bad about not being perfect?** (One answer might be, "You've grown some, but keep pressing on. God is working in you, and He will keep working in you if you let Him.") **We can acknowledge our sins and flaws and learn from them without dwelling on them. Instead of being discouraged by the gap between us and perfection, we can see it as hopeful and a challenge. Christ has a lot of work to do in our lives, and He can be counted on to do it! What does Philippians 1:6 promise?** (That God has started this work of growing us spiritually, and will keep doing it until the end.) Sometimes it may not look that way, but He keeps His Word.

---

*T*rusting God to complete what He has started in our lives. Hand out activity piece E2 ("Progress Report"). Have kids rate themselves in the areas listed. Give them time to ponder, since some will find it hard to evaluate themselves. When kids have completed their evaluations, let volunteers share the results. Do they seem to be getting "better" or "worse"? Point out that we need to measure ourselves against the example of Jesus; other Christians who know us well can also help us know how we need to grow and when we're making progress.

This group of qualities is called the "fruit of the Spirit" (Galatians 5:22, 23). How is growing fruit like "growing" these qualities? (It takes time to grow them; the Holy Spirit is like a gardener who grows the fruit in us; we need to prepare ourselves as we would good soil or take care of ourselves as we would healthy trees in order to produce fruit; we can't force the fruit to grow—it comes naturally from our relationship with God.)

If we insist on perfection here and now—either in others or in ourselves—we're going to be very frustrated. Stay close to God, as a tree has to stay close to the soil, and you'll grow. God has promised it.

Allow students to silently reflect on this question: "Will I trust God to continue making me what He wants me to be, even if I still don't always like what I am?" Then pray together, committing your "perfecting" to the Lord. Thank Him for what He has done for you already. Offer to continue praying for anyone who is still struggling to accept himself or herself.

Sandy Larsen is a free-lance writer in Ashland, Wisconsin. She has worked with both senior and junior high youth in churches, camps, and street evangelism. Her publications include several Bible study books for youth.

4. Ripening Fruit

(Self-evaluation)
10-15 min.

1

The Impossible Dream

Using photos cut from magazines, have kids create composite versions of the ideal man and ideal woman (have girls create the ideal woman and boys the ideal man). Talk about how few people look like these "impossible dreams"—even the models in the magazines aren't perfect. How desirable is it for a Christian to be, or want to be, an impossible dream? What are the effects of constantly being presented with these ideals?

2

Like Father, Like . . .

Parents are famous for saying, "When I was your age . . ." Teens are famous for plugging their ears at those times. But this time, assign kids to ask their parents, "What *were* you like at my age?" Have kids write down the descriptions—height, weight, hair color, complexion, hobbies, performance in school, dreams, personality, etc. Kids should then answer the same questions about themselves—and compare the answers with those of their parents. What are the similarities? Differences? Which traits seem to run in the family? Which changed with age? How have parents dealt with their "unlovable" traits? This exercise could be done at a parent-teen gathering, or as a family project at home. Have volunteers tell the rest of the group how these bits of family history could improve the way they see themselves.

3

Creation/Destruction

Have each student make a simple human figurine out of clay, paper, chenille wires, even clothespins. Then have another student destroy each creation while the maker watches. Ask: How does it feel to see your creation ruined? Explain how God loves each person He has created, and that He grieves when we are hurt or destroyed—by each other or by ourselves. Use this illustration when you explain that our ultimate value lies in the fact that God has created and loves us.

BY SANDY LARSEN

4
Unwritten Laws

Have kids compile lists of the unwritten laws at their schools—things everybody knows you can, can't, or *have* to do. For example: If you date the same person twice you're going steady; if you don't drink you won't get elected to any class office (or if you *do* drink you won't get elected); you have to have a car to be anybody; a guy can wear one earring but not two; you have to have so-and-so's records (or, you're out of it if you're still listening to so-and-so's records). Talk about the pressure caused by these unwritten laws that can affect the way we see ourselves.

5
Advertise For Good

As a group, go through magazines and make a montage of ad messages that reflect *good* and *lasting* values. They will probably be rare; kids may have to creatively combine several ads to form a message about what God wants us to do with our lives. Rewriting ads in this way will help kids see that they can reject or change identity-warping messages rather than swallowing them whole.

6

Compliment Exchange

To boost self-images, have kids write one complimentary, true thing about each person in the youth group. Collect the comments and put each recipient's notes in a sealed envelope to be opened in privacy. Or provide gift-wrapping materials so that kids can wrap compliments and present them to each other.

7
Unwritten Laws II

Have kids make lists like those in number 4, but this time the unwritten laws should be those of your own youth group. Discuss the effects of these pressures and expectations. Where do the rules come from? Do they prod kids to become mature in Christ? Do they encourage kids to act "spiritual" at the meetings and "worldly" the rest of the time? Do they make certain students feel like outsiders? How could following the rules affect the way you see yourself? How might rebellion against the rules affect you? Which rules need changing?

8

Mirror Count

For one day have kids count how many times they look at themselves in mirrors, including store windows and car windows. Then discuss their reasons for looking. How do they feel when they see themselves? Do they accept what they see, or are they desperate to change? Some teens may avoid looking in mirrors at all because they don't like what they see. Follow the discussion with a study of Genesis 1 and 2, paying particular attention to the way God sees His creation—as "very good."

9

Peer Pull

Have a larger student stand on a chair and a smaller student stand in front of him. As they grasp each other's hands, the one on the chair will try to pull the smaller one up, and the one on the floor will try to pull the larger one down. The smaller kid will probably win. Talk about how we have to be constantly on guard against being "pulled" by peers—because it's easier to get pulled down by others than to be lifted up.

10

Animal Identity

Find out how group members see themselves by asking each person to complete this sentence: "The animal I remind myself of most is . . ." Follow up with another sentence completion: "If I could be any animal, I would be . . ." Discuss the characteristics each person sees in himself or herself now, and those desired.

11

TV Watch Night

Gather the group for an evening of critical TV watching. Change channels frequently to see a wide range of programming. Provide bells, horns, or other noisemakers for kids to use when a show or commercial holds up as ideal a way of looking or behaving (wearing this makeup, looking like that star, acting like this macho hero, etc.). Kids will have to pay close attention to catch the implied messages, especially if they have been taking TV values for granted. Stop to discuss these identity formers every 15 minutes or so.

12

Tie-Up

Use this object lesson when discussing how peer pressure affects our ability to discover who we are. With light chains, tie a few students' hands together, either in front of them or behind their backs. Let them try to function for a while that way; then release them. (The most dramatic way would be to cut their chains.) Talk about how we are chained to other people's opinions when we let them decide how we will live and what kind of people we will be. Christ breaks those chains and frees us to do the right thing no matter what anyone else thinks.

13

Plenty of Time

Kids may be better able to live with their imperfections when they remember that their lives are eternal—which gives them plenty of time to grow and to be perfected by God. In other words, today is the first day of the rest of their eternal lives. You can illustrate this concept with an "eternal time line." Make a conventional time line— a horizontal line on a large sheet of paper or cardboard, with "1900" written at the left end and "1995" at the right—and hang it at the front of the room. Have kids mark on the line the years they've lived so far, and sign their names on their "lifetimes." Mark and sign yours, too. Then attach a long piece of brightly colored yarn or crepe paper to "1995"and extend the line all the way around the room, ending up back at "1900." Have kids compare the length of their lives so far with yours, with the average earthly lifetime, and with the "length" of eternity. Brainstorm some of the changes God could make in them, since He has forever to make them.

14

The Girl That I Marry

Have girls make a list of the characteristics they'd like to see in the ideal husband. Have boys do the same for wives. Make the lists available for the opposite sexes to read. They may find some surprises in the personal qualities that are actually valued by the opposite sex. Compare these ideals with common stereotypes of "good-looking babes" desired for dates. In addition to strengthening some self-images, this exercise can help teens realize that they themselves value deeper qualities in others than physical attractiveness and sexiness.

15

Sandwich Art

Have a "creative sandwich" party. Provide all kinds of usual and unusual fixings so that students can create wild and exotic sandwiches. Present a prize for the most unusual one (with the winner student-selected). Stipulate that students must eat the sandwiches they make! Discuss the imagination used in the project and talk about how God's creativity is unimaginably more than ours. He has created all sorts of people, each of them valuable in His sight. He can also think of countless ways to help us in our identity searches.

16

Puppet Pressure

The whimsy of puppets sometimes enables them to discuss subjects mere humans can't. Ask several students to come up with a puppet skit that sheds light on sexual pressures teens face. Suggestion: One puppet character could pressure the other with a series of "lines" commonly used by kids at school (such as, "Everybody does it," "If you really loved me, you'd show me," etc.). The pressured puppet could point out the falsehoods in each line, resisting the temptation to be a "puppet" of others. Assist the scriptwriters as needed, and provide puppets and a performing area. After the show, discuss the difficulties and rewards of having a strong identity in Christ rather than turning into a puppet under pressure.

17

Thankfulness Meeting

Set aside time for group members to thank God for the things that make up their lives and identities. They can do this out loud, in writing, or both. Lead them to think about people and things they're thankful for: parents, home, food, church, friends, talents. Encourage them to make detailed lists of blessings, including what's in their rooms, things friends have said to them, good times they've had, problems the Lord has helped them through. This exercise in thankfulness can be a great uplift for your kids—and you!

19
Special People

Bring your kids face-to-face with those who have confronted unusual challeges in their identity formation—the disabled. A burn victim, for example, must look beyond physical beauty to discover who he or she is; those in wheelchairs can't count on athletic ability to give them a sense of value. Some mentally retarded persons, unable to perform "normal" tasks, have learned to see the truly important things about themselves, others, and God. If some in your group are disabled, give them the opportunity to share their struggles and insights. If not, your group could visit an institution or have a few disabled people as guests. You'll probably find the interaction moving as well as memorable.

18
Old-Fashion Show

Stage a fashion show in which your teen models wear outdated clothes from 1960-1980 (check secondhand stores, school drama departments, and parents' closets for these). Accompany the showings with gushy commentary on these "hip, now, up-to-date" looks. After your group has a good laugh at these blasts from the past, point out how important it was for kids from those periods to dress in these clothes in order to be accepted. Have kids describe what's "in" and "out" at the moment. What are the dangers of "dressing for success"? How can they form strong identities apart from changing fashions?

20
Creativity Night

To celebrate God's creativity in making each of us unique, plan a Creativity Night at which students have the opportunity to express themselves through art, music, poetry, or any other form you wish. Bring in resource people from your church or community who can explain fundamentals of drama, creative writing, drawing, baking, pottery making, songwriting, or other arts or crafts. Let students present their creations to others if they wish. Explain at the beginning that this event is not a competition but a celebration, and that all members' creations are to be accepted uncritically as their expressions of what God has placed in them.

Sandy Larsen is a free-lance writer in Ashland, Wisconsin. She has worked with both senior and junior high youth in churches, camps, and street evangelism. Her publications include several Bible study books for youth.

Coping with Cliques

How to help your kids choose real security over the false security cliques offer

BY GARY W. DOWNING

I hadn't seen most of the people in 20 years. But while attending my high school reunion, I was surprised to find that I was feeling some of the same things I'd felt as a student. It was as if no time had passed.

When I saw Maggie, the girl who hit me in the head with her lunch box in the third grade, I felt the same dislike I'd once felt toward her. When I saw Andy, the guy who beat me out for quarterback in football and defeated me in class elections, I experienced the same rush of jealousy and hurt I'd felt as a high school senior.

Most striking, however, was the fact that those who had been in the "elite" clique as kids still grouped together at the reunion. I felt as excluded as I had 20 years before. It was a sharp reminder that not only teenagers hang out in cliques.

The challenge of coping with cliques is not confined to youth groups. Whatever the setting, the very nature of cliques is opposed to Jesus' call to an inclusive community. What can you do about cliques that emerge in your group?

The Need to Belong

Most cliques are created by our deep-seated psychological need to belong. We actually feel deprived if we can't claim a group as our own. So we'll do almost anything to be included. But then a strange thing happens: We forget what it was like to be outside the group. It's as if we close a door behind us, fearing that if we allow others to come in, they will somehow threaten our position in the group.

We gain esteem and security in a group, but we may also experience a loss of personal identity. We tend to give up our individuality for the security a clique offers, which hampers our ability to make our own moral decisions. In spite of deep beliefs, our personal values and behavior often become mirrors of the group. For teenagers who are forming their own identity, the pressure to conform is tremendous—and potentially devastating to their growth.

Offering Real Security

We generally can't break up dangerous cliques by threatening them. The positive aspects of cliques are so strong in kids' minds that, given a choice, they will often choose to remain in the clique even if it means alienation from the larger group. So what can we do? How can we go beyond condemning cliques that give kids false security and offer *real* security without the loss of identity? How can we create a climate that allows a group to be open ended, inclusive, and affirming of Biblical beliefs and values?

Here are four ideas that might help you better cope with cliques in your group:

1. *Provide opportunities for shared experiences in your group.* When your group arrives, sits, and leaves without real interaction, many members may find their security threatened. They will pull even more tightly into cliques to meet their psy-

chological needs. Instead of attacking the cliques, offer experiences that will help break down interpersonal barriers. Low-skill competition games, fun times together, or service projects in an unfamiliar environment can help foster communication and build relationships. Demonstrate how kids can trust and feel secure *outside* their cliques.

2. *Encourage group members to change their traffic patterns.* As flexible as young people appear, their lives are often very ordered and insulated. They will sit at the same lunch table every day with the same old group and even follow the same paths to their lockers and classes. A teenager might never see two-thirds of the other students in high school because of the ruts he follows. Cliques can form just by defining their "turf" among the lunch tables at school, or even in the youth room at church.

Challenging kids to change their traffic patterns "just for fun" for one week might help expose them to other students who feel even more insecure than they do. In one suburban group, we actually made a "contract" after discussing the concept of the outsider from the story of the Good Samaritan. We contracted to go out of our way to a different part of the lunchroom or the school building once each day, just to see what it was like. Natural curiosity plus prayerful encouragement made the experiment a real eye-opener. Kids had not realized what cliquish creatures of habit they had become. We then talked about the nature of

real security and how to experience it inside, even when the external environment is different. The experiment provided some fresh perspectives about why cliques develop and how to take a first step toward opening them up.

3. *Try to reach the leader.* Working with an inner-city gang, I realized that the clique leader is often the *most* ripe for a change. Having gained increased esteem by becoming the leader, he or she may feel empty at the top. I discovered a real feeling of boredom behind the bravado of one gang leader. Sure, it was nice to have people looking to him for direction, but it was lonely, too. With whom could he share his real feelings as long as he had a facade to maintain? We had to meet in private over a period of time to really come to grips with the underlying feelings my young gang leader friend was unable to express to his clique. Eventually he gained enough security in our friendship and in his faith to make a change.

4. *Help your group turn outward.* The main difference between an exclusive clique and an inclusive fellowship is the direction the group is facing. Picture a ring of people holding hands, standing shoulder to shoulder, facing inward, responding in unison to one member only. Any outsider trying to break into the circle is confronted by cold, hard backs. Then picture a ring of people also holding hands, standing shoulder to shoulder, but facing outward. They can no longer all look at one member of the cir-

cle for direction. Instead, they can see the outsider as a person to be welcomed instead of a threat to be repelled. That's an analogy of real Christian community. Try circling your group each way to model the differences, then talk about the various feelings the kids had.

Called to Care

——— ■ ———

Christ calls us to commitment, to community, and to caring for the outsider. Christ also gives us a new basis for real security that is expressed in a group, but also transcends the group. May He give you the power to model the kind of love needed to help your group establish a firm focus and foundation. □

Dr. Gary W. Downing *is executive minister of the Colonial Church of Edina, Minnesota. Formerly he was executive director for Youth Leadership and was part of the National Training Staff for Young Life.*

BY STEVE AND ANNIE WAMBERG

The Somebody Syndrome

Characters

■

Bland Betty (or Bob)

The Artsies

The Jocks

The Brains

The Trendies

Sam (or Samantha) Body

The Artsies, Jocks, Brains, and Trendies may be individuals or small groups, depending on the number of actors available.

Props

■

Each group (Artsies, Jocks, etc.) needs a trunk, suitcase, or paper bag in which to carry its props. Here are prop suggestions.

Artsies: paint palette, fake nose and mustache, band instrument, dance shoes

Jocks: football, volleyball, tennis shoes, sweat socks

Brains: eyeglasses, stack of books, computer disks

Trendies: latest, most outlandish fashions and hair accessories

Costumes

■

Bland Betty or Bob: White (or other bland color) T-shirt and pants
Groups: Clothing appropriate for their stereotypes
Sam: regular school clothes

The Play

———■———

As the action begins, Bland Betty or Bob (BB) is near center stage, surrounded (but not obscured) by the groups.

BB *(blandly at first, to audience)*: Hi. I'm Bob [Betty]. I'm bland. They call me Bland Bob [Betty]. I am on a quest to find out who I am. To boldly go where no man has gone before. But I'm a little confused, 'cause, uh, since no man has gone there before, how do I get there? I mean, on the highways of life, what road do I take? Like, hey—who am I? *(pauses, looks toward ARTSIES)* Yo! Yonder comes someone who doesn't look bland at all. Maybe he [she] can help me find out who I am.

ARTSIES (A) *(approaching BB)*: Hmmmm . . . There's someone who would make a great still life painting. I mean—he's [she's] so *bland*!

BB: Do you think you could help me, Bland Bob [Betty], become, uh, unbland? You look like you know who you are.

A *(pleased that he noticed)*: Yes. I am . . . artsy. I express who I am by drawing—or writing a poem—oh, and painting, or being in plays—and don't forget music.

BB *(pointing at suitcase)*: Hey—got anything in there that would fit someone like me?

A: Sure! *(Reaches into suitcase and begins pulling out things and handing them to BB. Leaves some things lying on the stage.)* There. That ought to make you into somebody! *(Turns and goes back to original place as BB picks up paint palette and tries on fake nose and mustache.)*

BB *(as if it's a limerick):* I've found myself! What an easy thing! I guess my quest is over. So now I think I'll head right home and sketch my old dog, Rover! *(Turns to leave but is stopped by the approach of the JOCKS.)*

JOCKS (J): Oh, how boring.

BB: What do you mean?

J: If you were really somebody, you'd be a jock. Yeah. You'd play sports.

BB: Not draw, act, sing, or dance?

J: Naw. Look, I think I can help you. *(Reaches into suitcase and hands items to BB.)*

BB: A jock, huh? *(Puts down artsy things to take hold of athletic props.)* So I'm a jock . . .

J: You made it, kid! How's it feel? *(Exits as BB answers.)*
BB: Actually, it feels okay. I think I'll go home and have some Wheaties. Yeah, that's the ticket! *(Turns to leave, but is cut off by the approach of BRAINS.)*

BRAINS (BRN): I have intercepted rumor of your most imposing quest and have come to set your mind at ease by showing you that true self is found in—

BB *(tossing football in the air)*: But you're—a brain!

BRN: Indubitably. That's what I've been trying to tell you. True self is found in knowledge!

BB: Aww, I don't have time for that. I have to be at practice as soon as I eat my Wheaties.

BRN: Pray, suspend such subcerebral behavior for a moment. Let me show you . . . a book. *(Removes other objects from BB's hands, opens suitcase, takes out a book, and hands it to BB.)*

BB: Huh? *(Starts to read and gets excited.)* Got any more? This is great!

BRN *(handing another to BB)*: Try this one!

BB *(flipping through pages as if speed-reading)*: This is—splendid! It's stupendous! It is truly a wondrous thing to have knowledge and to luxuriate in the increase of same!

BRN: Aptly put. *(Piles more books in BB's arms. Takes out glasses and puts them on BB; hands over calculator.)* That ought to hold you for a while! *(Exits to original place as BB says next line.)*

BB: Ah, to find myself in books. To unlock my future through the accumulated wisdom written by sages of old . . . *(Begins to exit but is cut off by TRENDIES.)*

TRENDIES (T): Oh! How totally gross!

BB: Excuse me?

T: It is just so *gagmatic* that you have all those books. I mean, if you read all those things, when will you have time to eat the right foods, like seaweed pizza? Or have time to shop for the latest fashions? In order to be a really happening person, you need to always be aware of what's hot and what's not. You know?

BB: But my books . . . It sounds like your suggestions would demand my full-time attention.

T: Totally. For sure. Here, I'll help you get started. *(Takes the books out of BB's arms and opens suitcase. After throwing a few things over shoulder in digging through contents, pulls out some clothes and accessories and hands them to BB.)* Put these on and in no time you'll be a cool dude [blazing fox], a happening individual—a trendie. *(Exit to original position as BB says next lines.)*

BB: Awesome. I can feel the vibes—I can't wait to get to the mall! *(Starts to walk away but trips on items that are lying on the stage. Falls, sits. Notices items from each group and picks them up fondly, one at a time—then stops.)* Hey, wait a minute! Am I a jock, a trendie, a brain, or an artsy person? Now I'm more confused than ever . . .

SAM (S) *(walking toward BB while speaking and looking at items on floor)*: Whoa! A garage sale!

BB *(Looking up suddenly.)*: Who are you?

S: My name's Body. Sam Body. But everyone just calls me Sam.

BB: Then *you're* somebody!

S: No, *Sam* Body.

BB *(disappointed)*: Oh, then you're *not* somebody.

S: No more than you are.

BB: What's that supposed to mean?

S: What do *you* think it means to be somebody?

BB: Well . . . the Trendies told me I should stay current on what was cool; then I'd be somebody. But the Jocks told me sports would make me into somebody. But the Brains said it's what you *know* that makes you a person. But what about being able to express who you are through the arts? I guess I just don't know what a somebody is.

S: What you choose to do with yourself is important, but it may not answer your question.

BB *(disappointed again):* Ohh . . . I suppose this is one of those searches that never ends or something like that, right?

S: The *adventure* doesn't have to end. But your frustration could ease up a little.

BB: Really? How?

S: You've been concentrating on how you look and what activities you enjoy. There's another question to be asked.

BB: Like, "Who am I?"

S: Right! Why don't you ask the Somebody Maker? The One who makes everybody anybody in the first place. He thought you were somebody before you started asking questions about it. He didn't make any nobodies.

BB: Then I *am* somebody. But I can't carry all this stuff around. Still, I like to play football. And I like to read. And I even think it's okay to draw and stuff like that. I probably like seaweed pizza, too. Am I warped?

S: You just sound well rounded. You're finding out who you are and what you like.

BB: Well, then, I'm not bland anymore! From now on I'll be *Blend* Bob [Betty]. Yeah, *that's* the ticket! I *will* boldly go where no man has gone before!

ALL *(unison):* And the adventure continues!

CURTAIN

Steve and Annie Wamberg *are the founders of Harvesthome Productions, an evangelistic arts and research organization. They perform concerts of original music, comedy, drama, and puppetry. They are also contributors to the award-winning* Young Teen Action *series (David C. Cook Publishing Co.).*

Lifted Up!

Photo by Michael Goldberg

A RETREAT AFFIRMING WHO WE ARE AS CHILDREN OF GOD

Breakaway

Aim

BY DICK HARDEL

To provide an opportunity for youth and their leaders to affirm each other as God's special children, and to experience the "lift" of the Holy Spirit who is working in their lives.

Overview

Sometimes we stumble in our Christian lives and get discouraged about who we are and how we have failed. Teens are especially vulnerable to despair as they struggle with distorted self-images and search for their unique identities. This retreat is designed to give kids helpful affirmation of who they are as special individuals created by a loving God. Through the Holy Spirit and the encouragement of other believers, God can make us new again, free again, and alive again.

You'll Need

□ Bibles
□ pencils, paper
□ Need a Lift? (activity piece BR1 from the back of this book)
□ uplifting theme song for the retreat, plus other songs to sing
□ construction paper, newsprint, markers, scissors, stapler
□ blank kites, materials to decorate them, kite string
□ Christian music tapes and good tape player
□ ribbon or strips of cloth for kite tails
□ varied materials for kids' self-portraits
□ Scripture Lift (activity piece BR2)
□ balloons

Optional:
□ slides of kids, projector(s), cords
□ weather balloon and compressor to inflate it
□ Christian film, projector, screen
□ helium tank and fitting for filling balloons
□ cards to attach to balloons
□ equipment and elements for celebration of the Lord's Supper

SCHEDULE

Friday

	Pre-retreat worship event
8:00 p.m.	Arrive and get settled
8:30 p.m.	Name Wall
9:00 p.m.	Kite creations
10:00 p.m.	Break
10:30 p.m.	Wrap-up
11:30 p.m.	Free time
Midnight	Rest well

Noon	Lunch
1:00 p.m.	Emmaus walk
1:30 p.m.	Kite flying
2:30 p.m.	Free time
6:00 p.m.	Supper
7:00 p.m.	Singing, fun time
8:00 p.m.	Self-Portraits
9:00 p.m.	Break
9:30 p.m.	Bible balloons
10:30 p.m.	Wrap-up
11:30 p.m.	Rest well

Saturday

7:00 a.m.	Scripture time
8:00 a.m.	Breakfast
9:00 a.m.	Christian music moments
9:15 a.m.	Singing
9:30 a.m.	"Need a Lift" Bible study
10:45 a.m.	Break
11:00 a.m.	Affirmation tails

Sunday

7:00 a.m.	Scripture time
8:00 a.m.	Breakfast
9:00 a.m.	Christian music moments
9:30 a.m.	Worship preparation
10:30 a.m.	Worship celebration
11:30 a.m.	Clean up, pack up
Noon	Journey home

Retreat Activities

— ∎ —

Pre-Retreat Worship

Before leaving for the retreat, have your kids meet at the church for a brief worship event. Make copies of "Need a Lift?" (activity piece BR1 from the back of this book) and have youth and adults read the parts. If you can't do it before you leave, you might want to use the activity as your first at the retreat site.

Choose a theme song for your retreat ahead of time. Sing it to wrap up your worship time together. Then pray together for a safe trip and a refreshing, enriching weekend.

Name Wall

Instruct each person (including adults) to choose a positive, self-descriptive adjective which begins with the first letter of his or her name—as in Joyous Jill, Mechanical Mike, Big Bill, etc. Go around the circle, having each person say his or her new nickname and repeating, in order, each nickname already given.

Then cover one large area of a wall with newsprint. Using felt-tip pens, kids should write their nicknames on the wall. But all names are to be joined in crossword style.

Kite Creations

If you can't find or make blank kites for this kite-decorating activity, they can be purchased from S & S Arts and Crafts, Colchester, CT 06415.

First, have kids write their first names large enough on their kites that their names can be read from a long distance. Then have kids write (in smaller letters) all the strengths they see in themselves—creative, tall, humorous, caring, etc.—and add any decorations they wish from the materials you've made available.

When kites are done, divide kids into small groups to share what they've written on the kites. Kids should then write on each other's kites the strengths they see in one another.

Let the group know you'll be flying the kites the next day if weather permits. You'll be making tails for the kites tomorrow morning. Wrap up this session by having kids thank God for all the strengths and gifts He has given them. If possible, hang kites on the wall where everyone can see them.

Evening Wrap-up Options

Personal Slide Show

Help your kids celebrate who they are as persons God has made. Sometime before the retreat, take lots of slides of your kids at different activities (ten slides of each kid would not be too many). Have those slides ready to show for this event.

If possible, inflate a large weather balloon to use as a projection screen. Have kids "lift each other up" by bouncing the balloon gently around the room above their heads while you hold the projector and keep it aimed at the floating balloon. Have hymns or songs of praise playing on a record player or tape recorder. Overhead lights should be turned off or dimmed. Since weather balloons can break easily, tell kids to bounce the balloon very gently. If you can use two projectors and keep them directed at the balloon from different sides of the room, the effect will be even more interesting. Keep changing the slides during the music.

It might be a good idea to experiment with this slide show before the retreat to make sure everything works. Weather balloons can be purchased from the Edmund Scientific Company, 101 East Gloucester Pike, Barrington, New Jersey 08007.

When your slide show is over, close this activity by thanking God for making each of your kids just the way He did.

Other Options

If you're in a situation where you can have a campfire, enjoy it! Have kids sing or listen to music, and encourage them to share their expectations for the weekend. Or you could show a good film to wrap up the evening. Be sure it's not too heavy, and that it will be affirming for kids, not guilt producing.

Want a brief devotional before kids go to bed? Use one or two of the Scripture passages used in activity piece BR1. Discuss with kids the meaning of the passage and let them apply it to their lives.

Scripture Time

The early morning Scripture time is a special quiet time to get ready for the day. It is a time of morning offering—an opportunity to offer the whole day to the Lord. Encourage everyone to read and meditate on Psalm 24 or 27 (or both) for several minutes, offering the day to the Lord.

Christian Music Moments

Try playing Christian music that your kids enjoy. Music can have a real ministry to them. You might want to let kids bring their own tapes. Music times in the schedule are designed for creative listening; after a song or set of songs, try dividing the group into threes or fours to discuss the music's messages.

Need a Lift? Bible Study (Ephesians 4:11-16)

Divide kids into groups of five or six and pass out pencils and paper. Instruct each kid to draw a gift-wrapped box to represent himself or herself.

Think of three things you do well. These are gifts God has given you. Using creative symbols, draw those gifts in the box. Then share your drawings with the members of your small group. Give kids some time for drawing and discussing before you move on.

Continue thinking of yourself as a gift. What are you wrapped up in? How do people know what gifts are in you? Share your answers with your group.

After kids have talked, read Ephesians 4:11-16 aloud. Then, as a group, discuss the following questions:

- **Why did God give us people with so many different kinds of gifts?**
- **How does this passage say those gifts are important?**
- **What does Christ do in all of this?**
- **How can people be gifts to us?**
- **How can we be gifts to other people?**

Now have kids write on the gift box the names of two people who have been like gifts to them at some point in their lives. Also, have them write down the name of a person to whom they may have been gifts in some way. Have kids talk about these special people in their small groups. Then discuss the following questions in the larger group:

- **How does it make you feel to know you may already have been like a gift to someone else?**
- **How does it make you feel to know that God has a special purpose and place for you?** (Don't let kids just say, "Great!" Press them for more specific feelings.)

Close by joining in a circle prayer, thanking God for the gifts He has given and for all the members of your group.

Affirmation Tails

Pass out ribbon or strips of cloth for kids to use as tails for the kites decorated earlier. Have each teen make an "affirmation bow" for the tail of every other kid's kite—as well as one for his or her own. Bows should be cut from construction paper, and a note of affirmation written on each one. Notes should begin with a phrase like, "What I like best about you, Bill, is. . ." If you have more than 15 people, you may want to divide into smaller groups and just have kids make bows for those in their own groups.

When bows are finished, have everyone sit in a circle. Put a chair in the middle and choose one person to start by sitting in the chair. Then have each person read the affirmation bow they wrote for the person in the chair and give it to him or her.

Proceed until all have had a turn in the center chair. Then have kids staple their affirmation bows to the tails of their kites.

If weather permits, go out and fly the kites. If not, fly them the next morning or attach them to the ceiling or wall of the main meeting room for everyone to see.

Emmaus Walk

Have your kids go for half-hour walks in pairs or groups of three. During this time they are to look for signs of God's presence and talk about where they are in their faith, seeking to build one another up as brothers and sisters in Christ.

Self-Portraits

Give your kids a chance to express who they are through whatever means they choose. Have each kid create some kind of portrait of himself or herself in 30 minutes. Kids may want to center on their accomplishments or talents, or just describe themselves in general through drawings, sculpture, taped monologues, songs, or other means. Have group members explain their portraits and give each other a round of applause. Then thank God for the gifts He's given kids.

Bible Balloons

For your closing activity Saturday night, divide kids into groups of three to six. Ahead of time, cut out the Scripture passages from "Scripture Lift" (activity piece BR2), fold them up small, and insert them into balloons. Blow up and tie the balloons. If you have more slips of paper than kids, make sure you give out close to equal numbers of the various Bible passages. If you have more kids than slips, photocopy extra slips as needed.

Give each teen one balloon. Then read Psalm 150 aloud. Have kids rattle their balloons whenever an instrument of praise is mentioned. After reading the last verse ("Let everything that has breath praise the Lord. Praise the Lord"), have kids pop their balloons, read the Bible passages, and find the people who have the same passage as they have. When they have found their partners, have them sit in groups and discuss what that passage means to them. Close by singing a quiet song of praise.

Sunday Worship

Use all your kids to help plan the worship service. Center it on the theme, "God Gives a Lift!" You may want to give a brief talk using Acts 1:6-11. If your church allows it in such a setting, a celebration of the Lord's Supper might be appropriate.

For an exciting conclusion, have helium-filled balloons prepared that morning before your worship celebration (check the yellow pages in your phone book for sources of helium and rental of equipment). Give kids small cards (about business card size) on which to write messages of praise to God for what He has done for them this weekend. Also have each teen write his or her name and address on the back of the card and attach it to a helium balloon with a string. Release the balloons together with shouts or songs of praise in celebration of God's goodness. Not only will this be a memorable wrap-up to the weekend, but the excitement may continue for several weeks as some of the balloons are found and the cards returned. □

Dr. Dick Hardel *is associate pastor, St. John's Lutheran Church, Winter Park, Florida. Dick has been involved in youth ministry since 1970 and each year designs scores of retreats.*

MY EULOGY

(What my best friend would probably say about me if I died—to be spoken at a memorial service in front of the entire student body of my school.)

The most important person in my life was: _____

My best friends were:

_____

My favorite thing to do was:

_____

My favorite place to be alone was:

_____

My worst habit was:

_____

The ugliest thing about me was:

_____

The thing I feared most was:

_____

My greatest accomplishment was:

_____

The most important thing in my life was: _____

What I hoped to do with my life was:

_____

My teachers remembered me as:

_____

My minister remembered me as:

_____

My coach remembered me as:

_____

God remembered me as:

_____

Three characteristics of my life were:

_____

THE SELLING OF

SLUDGE

A VERY SHORT PLAY

Characters:

J. T. Blubwell, company big shot
Nitly, his assistant
Ms. Fleem, another assistant

The Place: J. T. Blubwell's office

J. T.: Why, these sales reports are terrible! (Picking up imaginary phone) Nitly! Get in here right away!

Nitly (entering timidly): Uh, yes, Mr. Blubwell?

J. T.: Nitly, the Sludge Corporation is in big trouble! Here we are producing buckets and buckets of this disgusting, slimy Sludge, and we can't sell it! That's your job, Nitly—to sell Sludge!

Nitly: B-but—but nobody likes Sludge, sir. It's—slimy and disgusting.

J. T.: That makes no difference, Nitly! You're supposed to get people to buy it. There must be *some* reason to buy Sludge!

Nitly: Uh . . . I can't think of any, sir.

J. T.: You're a nitwit, Nitly! (Picking up phone) Ms. Fleem! Get in here on the double!

Fleem (entering confidently): Yes, Mr. Blubwell?

J. T.: Fleem, I want answers. Tell me three things you can do with Sludge.

Fleem (thinking fast): You can . . . wear it on your head.

Nitly: Wear it on your *head?*

Fleem: Right. Just dump it on and stick feathers in it.

J. T.: Good, good! What else?

Fleem: You can . . . put it in your gas tank.

Nitly: *What?*

Fleem: And you can take a bath in it.

Nitly: A *bath?* I don't see why anybody would want to—

J. T.: Fleem, I like your style. Now, who are we going to convince to do all these things with Sludge?

Fleem: Teenagers, sir. We'll hit them with the biggest advertising campaign you've ever seen. We'll have Sludge T-shirts, headbands, Frisbees, music videos, and movie tie-ins. We'll sell them Sludge candy bars, Sludge perfume, and Sludge with benzoyl peroxide! We'll tell them that if they wear Sludge on their heads, they'll be popular. If they put it in their gas tanks, they'll get dates. If they take baths in it, they'll smell like Madonna.

Nitly: But what if they're *guys?*

Fleem: Then they'll smell like Sean Penn.

J. T.: Wonderful, splendid! But we need slogans, jingles!

Fleem: How about, "Sludge is it"? Or, "Sludge: The choice of a new generation"?

J. T.: I love it! Fleem, I'm putting you in charge of our new advertising campaign. And Nitly, I'm demoting you to janitor! You can start by cleaning that awful-looking stuff off the floor.

Nitly: But, sir—that's a pile of Sludge!

J. T.: I know! Yuck! I hate the stuff! Let's go, Ms. Fleem—I know a lovely little place for lunch. (As they all exit) How about, "You deserve a Sludge today"? Or, "Sludge—Ah, the smell of it!" Or . . .

CURTAIN

Who Says?

Read Matthew 5:1-12. Then explain in the space provided how each of the following messages is different from Jesus' ways to happiness (blessedness). In each case, tell which verses might apply.

A. "If you drink this pop, you'll have great times and be happy."

B. "You don't want people to think you're boring and old fashioned, do you? Wear these clothes and they won't."

C. "Use this lipstick, and guys will want you."

D. "Look at those nerds who don't know how to be cool. Don't associate with them. Join the kids who use our product."

E. "You're on your way to the top, and you don't need anybody to help you get there. Show the others where you're headed by driving a car like this."

F. "You only go around once in life, so you've got to grab for all the gusto you can."

G. "Sure, it's expensive—but you're worth it."

H. "Go see this movie. You'll love the way the hero gets revenge on the guys who set him up."

I. "Buy this album. It's the album of the year, which means everybody else has it, and the most important thing is to be like everybody else."

J. "Want to be as rich and successful as this model? Use this perfume/cologne."

UNDER Pressure?

Write your answers to the following questions and complete the sentence starters.

■ In what ways are your feelings about yourself affected by what others think or say about you?

■ How can your choices be badly influenced by what others say or think about you?

■ You feel peer pressure most when . . .

■ You can handle peer pressure best when . . .

Freedom Commitment

How do you want to respond to the gift of freedom God has given you? Answer by completing the following:

Because God has given me the gift of freedom, I want to use it properly by:

When I feel peer pressure to do something that I know God would not want me to do, I will remember who I am and whose I am, and then respond to the peer pressure by:

I will seek to learn what is pleasing to God by:

I will try not to let what other people say about me affect how I feel about myself by:

My Prayer
Write a prayer asking God to help you to fulfill the above commitment. Feel free to ask Him to help you with any specific problem or temptation you have.

How It All Got Started

Check the correct answer to each question based on Genesis 1:27, 28, 31 and 2:18-25. Be ready to tell why you agree or disagree with each (serious) option.

1. Who is made in the image of God?
   a. Women only.
   b. Men only.
   c. Men and women.
   d. Benedictine monks.

2. Adam's comment after Eve was made:
   a. Now we're in for it!
   b. Hide your credit cards!
   c. Now I've got a slave.
   d. This is very good!

3. What was not good?
   a. Sex.
   b. Apples.
   c. Man alone.
   d. Fig leaves.

4. The very first reason for sexuality was
   a. To end loneliness.
   b. To have children.
   c. To give parents something to worry about.
   d. To give teenagers something to worry about.

5. Woman was taken out of a man's side
   a. to walk alongside him.
   b. to emphasize their interrelatedness.
   c. to symbolically be near his heart.
   d. all of the above.

6. To be proud of my sexual identity as a man or woman is
   a. to be sexist.
   b. fine if I'm a woman, since Adam was a rough draft.
   c. to be walking in God's design.
   d. fine if I'm a man, since men are superior.

7. A real man
   a. recognizes he is complete when he is in relationship with the opposite sex.
   b. rejects a woman's advice.
   c. subdues the earth by himself.
   d. is supposed to name the children.

8. A real woman
   a. only lets the man *think* he is superior.
   b. is a partner in subduing and ruling over the earth.
   c. is barefoot, pregnant, and in the kitchen.
   d. succeeds when she is accepted as "one of the boys."

9. Men and women
   a. were created to have someone to argue with.
   b. only need each other for reproductive purposes.
   c. have nothing special to offer one another.
   d. are to bring their unique and special traits to their relationship.

Now, make up your own humorous question from the passage.

10.
   a.
   b.
   c.
   d.

Please Be Patient . . . God's Not Finished with Me Yet!

You've seen that reminder on T-shirts and plaques. It's a good message to give other Christians. But it's also a good message to give yourself. You're not perfect yet? Be patient with yourself . . . God's not finished with you yet!

"*In order to do all the things I want to do, I'll have to live to be a hundred!*"

Those words weren't spoken by a teenager. A lady over 80 years old said them! She had already lived a full life, but was looking forward to accomplishing more.

How about you? What would you like to do and be before you reach 100? Complete the "dream list" below.

I'd like to do . . .

I'd like to be . . .

PROGRESS REPORT

Rate yourself on a scale of 1 to 10 (10 is "absolutely perfect") in the following areas—as you were a year ago, as you are now, and as you might be a year from now if you and God work on it together.

	Last year	This year	Next year
I treat other people lovingly.			
I'm joyful.			
I'm at peace with myself and with God.			
I'm patient.			
I'm gentle with others.			
I want what God wants.			
My faith is strong.			
I'm more interested in others' needs than in my own.			
My self-control is in good shape.			

NEED A LIFT?

Leader: Well, the bus is loaded, we're only half an hour behind schedule, two people who said they were going aren't here, and five others are here unexpectedly. I guess I can handle it. I hope I'm prepared.

All: Need a lift?

Reader: (Read II Corinthians 12:9.)

Person 1: I get lost so easily in my faith. I'm not even sure I should be going on this retreat. I don't even know who I am. No one seems to care about me.

All: Need a lift?

Reader: (Read John 14:1-6.)

Person 2: Sometimes my life with Christ just loses flavor. I'm so common and ordinary that I bore myself. I don't think I'm worth anything. There's no way I could spice up anyone's life. I don't think God could use me.

All: Need a lift?

Reader: (Read Matthew 5:13a: "You are the salt of the earth.")

Person 3: Some mornings I want to pull the covers over my head and never get out of bed. There's nothing about me that is special to anyone. My parents never say a word to me. My dreams are the only place I ever shine.

All: Need a lift?

Reader: (Read Matthew 5:14-16.)

Person 4: If I had to choose a symbol to represent me, I'd choose a pancake. There are times when I feel run over by a freight train and my life in Christ is flat as a pancake.

All: Need a lift?

Reader: (Read I John 5:1-4.)

Person 5: I have never felt important. I never am chosen to do anything important. I don't know what my role is in the church. I just keep hoping to be discovered.

All: Need a lift?

Reader: (Read I Peter 2:9, 10.)

All: We are the people of God—His chosen people! And He'll give us the lift we all need!

Scripture Lift

II Timothy 1:12: "I know whom I have believed, and am convinced that he is able to guard what I have entrusted to him for that day."

Philippians 4:19: "My God will meet all your needs according to his glorious riches in Christ Jesus."

II Timothy 1:12: "I know whom I have believed, and am convinced that he is able to guard what I have entrusted to him for that day."

Philippians 4:19: "My God will meet all your needs according to his glorious riches in Christ Jesus."

Psalm 4:3: "Know that the Lord has set apart the godly for himself; the Lord will hear when I call to him."

Psalm 103:17: "From everlasting to everlasting the Lord's love is with those who fear him, and his righteousness with their children's children."

Psalm 4:3: "Know that the Lord has set apart the godly for himself; the Lord will hear when I call to him."

Psalm 103:17: "From everlasting to everlasting the Lord's love is with those who fear him, and his righteousness with their children's children."

Isaiah 12:2: "Surely God is my salvation; I will trust and not be afraid. The Lord, the Lord, is my strength and my song; he has become my salvation."

I John 1:9: "If we confess our sins, he is faithful and just and will forgive us our sins and purify us from all unrighteousness."

Isaiah 12:2: "Surely God is my salvation; I will trust and not be afraid. The Lord, the Lord, is my strength and my song; he has become my salvation."

I John 1:9: "If we confess our sins, he is faithful and just and will forgive us our sins and purify us from all unrighteousness."

Philippians 4:7: "And the peace of God, which transcends all understanding, will guard your hearts and your minds in Christ Jesus."

Ephesians 2:4, 5: "Because of his great love for us, God, who is rich in mercy, made us alive with Christ even when we were dead in transgressions."

Philippians 4:7: "And the peace of God, which transcends all understanding, will guard your hearts and your minds in Christ Jesus."

Ephesians 2:4, 5: "Because of his great love for us, God, who is rich in mercy, made us alive with Christ even when we were dead in transgressions."